New Orleans Voodoo

An Essential Guide to Louisiana Voodoo

Your Free Gift
(only available for a limited time)

Thanks for getting this book! If you want to learn more about various spirituality topics, then join Mari Silva's community and get a free guided meditation MP3 for awakening your third eye. This guided meditation mp3 is designed to open and strengthen ones third eye so you can experience a higher state of consciousness. Simply visit the link below the image to get started.

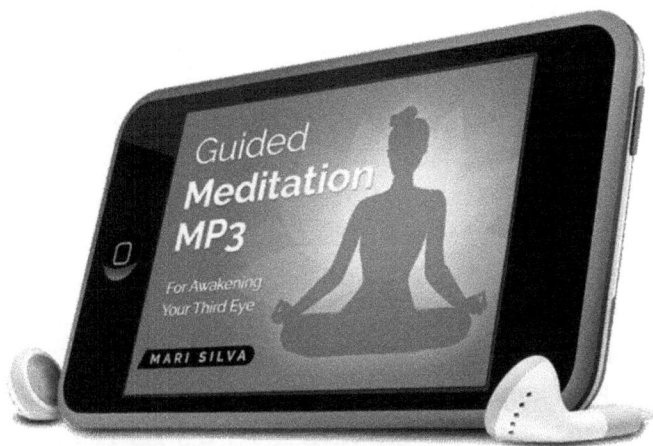

https://spiritualityspot.com/meditation

Table of Contents

Introduction

New Orleans Voodoo is a practice that has been shrouded in mystery and misconceptions for years. It is rather unfortunate that for many, the term Voodoo evokes images of black magic and human sacrifice, but the reality is that New Orleans Voodoo is a complex spiritual tradition with deep roots in the history and culture of Louisiana.

In this essential guide to Louisiana Voodoo, you're going to gain a deeper understanding of this powerful and often misunderstood practice. The book is perfect for both beginners who are just getting their feet wet when it comes to the powerful practice of New Orleans Voodoo and those who have some knowledge of Voodoo but want to delve deeper into their exploration of the tradition. You'll find this book is written in a clear and accessible style, making it easy to understand and follow along with the various practices and rituals.

There are many books on the subject out there, but you'll be glad you chose this one. What sets it apart from other similar guides is its hands-on approach. Rather than simply explaining the history and beliefs of New Orleans Voodoo, the book includes step-by-step instructions and practical advice on how to engage with the various rituals and practices. From creating your own altar to performing a Voodoo healing ceremony, readers will have everything they need to start their own Voodoo practice.

Another unique aspect of this book is its focus on the role of New Orleans in the development and spread of Voodoo. The city has long been a hub for spiritual practices and has played a vital role in preserving and evolving Voodoo in America. The book delves into the history of New Orleans and its various spiritual traditions, showing how Voodoo fits into this rich tapestry.

You will encounter the various spirits and deities central to New Orleans Voodoo. These include the powerful Loa, or spirits, which you can call upon for guidance, protection, and healing. The book explains the different types of Loa and their roles within the Voodoo tradition and provides guidance on how to work with them.

If you've always wanted a way to connect with the Divine, to deepen your roots in spirituality so that you can live a life with purpose and clarity, then this is definitely the path for you. It's not for those only looking to "curate" their lives to fit what they consider "aesthetic." It's for those who want to know the ancient ways, divine truths, and natural ways to live in harmony with one another. You'll discover all this and more as you read this book. If you're ready for your new spiritual journey, let's get into it.

Chapter One: What Makes New Orleans Voodoo Different?

Beliefs

West Africa is the cradle from which Voodoo sprung and grew. The word voodoo itself came about in Louisiana in 1850 and is considered a derivative of the French word voudou. Some say it's from the word vodu. You may find it spelled in a variety of other ways, like vodun, vodou, and so on.

For many reasons, the uninitiated or ignorant consider Voodoo to be the practice of black magic. Say the word "Voodoo," and it immediately brings to mind things like cursing people or sticking pins into a doll. But this is just a misrepresentation. Voodoo is all about the awareness that all things and all people are made of the same essence or Spirit. Therefore, everything is connected.

While Voodoo is from West Africa, it is rooted in Catholicism. As a syncretic religion, it is a mix of belief systems drawn from the Catholic Church and the West African Vodu ways. One of the fundamental ideas behind Voodoo is the fact that humans live in a world with spirits all around them. Humans aren't the only ones here. There are spirits known as Loa or Lwa, as well as the ancestors and angels, all of whom inhabit the worlds that cannot be seen with the naked eye. These spirits are so numerous that the Loa alone can be split into 17 pantheons, and there are over a thousand of them — some, admittedly more well-known than others.

Voodoo is rooted in Catholicism.
https://unsplash.com/photos/ZlIIA-4sGXU

According to Voodoo, all the spirits dwell in Ginen, and they were all made by Bondye, the Supreme Being who created all things seen and unseen. The purpose of these spirits is simple. They're supposed to act as assistants to Bondye, seeing to the affairs of the outside world. Not only that, but no one also gets to interact with Bondye directly other than these spirits. Therefore, if you have any petitions or prayers, they must go through the Loa. This isn't because Bondye doesn't care, but simply because the essence of Bondye is so different from humanity that the only way to communicate clearly and accurately with him is through the help of the Loa.

The practice of Voodoo isn't just something done now and then. It is a lifestyle, an awareness that each day is dedicated to the service of the Loa. Many practices are involved in this service, such as rites, rituals, special prayers, offerings, and more. These are all meant to get the Loa as involved in your daily affairs as possible, so they can bless you, help you figure out problems, keep you safe and healthy, and more. Those who practice Voodoo will dance and sing in honor of the Loa, and they also get into altered states of consciousness where the Loa themselves will possess them and use them to transmit messages or just demonstrate their presence to the people. Possession also allows those who practice

Voodoo to receive specific advice when needed.

Voodoo is a religious belief system rooted in spirituality and considers the ancestors to be an important aspect of life. Before analyzing what makes New Orleans Voodoo different from other forms of Voodoo, it is important to have a clear picture of the background of this amazing spiritual movement. So, here's a deep dive into the history and culture that led to the development of New Orleans Voodoo as it is known today.

Historical and Cultural Background

When it comes to Louisiana Voodoo, there is a lot of mystery shrouding its roots. In the year 1699, some French people arrived in the area and settled down. About 20 years later, the area would receive enslaved African people. Things remained relatively unchanged for over 40 years until the Spanish Empire stepped in and took over. They held the reins of power up until 1803. At this time, there was a synchronization of Catholicism that was the practice of the Spanish and the French, as well as the religions among those who had been enslaved in West Africa, and this served as the fertile ground from which Voodoo would spring.

All the people forced to leave West Africa knew a lot about various poisons, plants, herbal solutions, amulets, rituals, charms, and more. These were all used to keep themselves safe, and they would all eventually become a part of Louisiana or New Orleans Voodoo. When the French held sway, most Africans there were from the Senegal River basin. Specifically, they were of the Bambara tribe. There were other tribes as well, including the Dahomey people and the Kongolese. After the Spanish wrested power from the French, there were more and more Kongolese enslaved people. Naturally, there were soon far more enslaved people than white Europeans. Even before the enslaved people got there, the colony wasn't exactly a bastion of excellence and efficiency. Consequently, those who had only just arrived from sub-Saharan Africa would end up taking over the slave community.

Between 1731 and 1732, there were at least two African people for every European. Those Europeans involved in agriculture and the slave business weren't that great in number. One of the things that made it easier for Africans to prevent their culture from being overly diluted was the fact that the white people had ensured they would never interact with the Africans unless necessary. So this made it easier for the latter group to keep their culture as untainted as they could. This was more common in southern Louisiana than in the northern part of the state.

Because of Catholicism and the laws put in place by the French, it wasn't allowed to sell children of enslaved people off to other families if they weren't at least 14 years old. Since the people weren't being separated to be sold off, this made it easier for the bond between them to grow stronger, in addition to sharing a mutual understanding of what it's like not to have freedom.

An important part of New Orleans Voodoo is wearing amulets and other objects to stay safe from the elements and other people and heal themselves of any illnesses. For instance, there was the Ouanga, a potent charm that could be used on an enemy to poison them. Part of the ingredients for this charm were roots obtained from the African figuier maudit tree.

Eventually, Louisiana would come to be the property of the United States in the year 1803. This was around the time that the Africans in Saint-Domingue rose up to rid themselves of the terrorizing French colonials so that they could become the republic known today as Haiti. Some people chose to escape the war there and made their homes in Louisiana. They came with all they had, and that included Haitian Vodou, which was a result of the syncretization of Yoruba and Fon religious practices, as well as Roman Catholic ones. Enough people migrated so that New Orleans' population doubled; as they interacted with one another, many born in Louisiana chose to practice Voodoo. Not only that, but they also found a way to blend their practices with Haitian Voodoo, creating Louisiana Voodoo as it is known today. At this point in Louisiana Voodoo's history, it is important to look into the other branches of Voodoo that exist so that it's easier to demonstrate how these various branches differ from New Orleans Voodoo.

The Different Branches of Voodoo

Haitian Voodoo: Haitian Voodoo is perhaps the most well-known and widely practiced form in the Western world. It is a syncretic religion that combines elements of traditional West African religions, Catholicism, and indigenous beliefs. Haitian Voodoo is characterized by the veneration of ancestors, the use of spirit possession in rituals, and the use of drumming and dance as part of its religious practices. The religion also has a complex system of spirits, known as Lwa (Loa), who are believed to represent various aspects of the natural world and human experience.

A Haitian Voodoo altar.
https://www.flickr.com/photos/edk7/51102873969

African Voudou: African Voudou, on the other hand, is the oldest and most traditional form of Voodoo, with deep roots in West African cultures. It is a nature-based religion centered on worshiping deities known as Orishas, who represent various natural elements and forces. African Voudou emphasizes the importance of ancestor veneration, healing, and divination. Its rituals involve chanting, dancing, and drumming. Its practitioners often wear elaborate costumes and use symbolic objects during their ceremonies.

Hoodoo: Hoodoo, also known as "rootwork," is a practice of African American folk magic combining elements of African spirituality with Christian beliefs. Hoodoo practitioners use herbs, oils, and other ingredients to create potions and charms for various purposes, such as love, protection, and success. Hoodoo also incorporates divination and other forms of magic into its practice.

Louisiana Voodoo: Also called New Orleans Voodoo, this form developed in New Orleans. New Orleans Voodoo is a blend of African, European, and Native American spiritual traditions. It includes the worship of spirits, ancestor veneration, and the use of charms and spells. You're going to learn more about this form in this book.

Brazilian Vodou: Brazilian Vodou is also known as Candomblé. This is a religion that developed in Brazil and is heavily influenced by African spiritual practices. Brazilian Vodou involves the worship of Orishas, or deities, and includes a range of rituals and ceremonies.

Dominican Vodou: Also known as Las 21 Divisiones, Dominican Vodou is a form of Voodoo practiced in the Dominican Republic. Dominican Vodou involves the worship of spirits and includes a range of rituals and ceremonies.

Cuban Santeria: Cuban Santeria is sometimes called Lukumi. This is a religion that developed in Cuba and which is heavily influenced by African spiritual practices. Cuban Santeria involves the worship of Orishas, or deities, and includes a range of rituals and ceremonies.

When it comes to practicing all these forms of Vodou, personal beliefs also come into play, and, as a result, some people blend practices from the different forms of Vodou to create what resonates with them spiritually.

The Evolution of New Orleans Voodoo

It was only natural that, with time, New Orleans Voodoo would evolve to become something different, a conglomeration of different beliefs and practices from many spiritual traditions. Hoodoo, for instance, is a form of magic from South America. We can clearly find its fingerprints all over New Orleans Voodoo these days.

New Orleans Voodoo is still practiced because it is a true form of spirituality that connects you with the divine within and all around you. Many following this path are from the original Voodoo practitioners responsible for the religion. There are, however, a growing number of people who are not from New Orleans and do not have any connections with Voodoo but are very interested in the path. Some people are naturally drawn to it, so New Orleans Voodoo continues to spread. This is such a wonderful thing because, in the past, Voodoo was something most people demonized. These days, many people have come to not just recognize but accept it as a valid part of the culture of New Orleans.

When you consider the entire evolution of New Orleans Voodoo, it is hard to ignore the fact that it has continued to grow and adapt to the times and the beliefs of present-day practitioners. This spiritual way of life remains an intrinsic part of the city of New Orleans. The locals and visitors appreciate all its practices, history, and endurance.

Myths, Misconceptions, and Malicious Lies

It is a sad truth that once upon a time, Voodoo was heavily vilified, especially in popular culture. Many erroneously assumed that Voodoo was the same as evil black magic witchcraft or anything dark that one should not dabble with. The vilification of Voodoo is no accident. Some were deeply interested in discrediting Voodoo because of what they thought it stood for.

One of the major reasons that Voodoo is so misunderstood is because of its connection to the continent of Africa and the diaspora. You see, earlier in the 19th and 20th centuries, when Voodoo first became a thing in the Western world, many people had a terrible attitude towards people from Africa and their cultures. It was a time when racism and xenophobia reigned supreme. Looking through those lenses, those people naturally assumed that everything to do with Voodoo was barbaric and primitive. Anything and anyone associated with the practice was seen as ignorant. To these people, practitioners of Voodoo were savages. Therefore, ensuring this religion would not thrive and become a blemish upon their already established and lawful customs and cultures became very important to them.

Yet another incentive why these people had to vilify Voodoo is the fact that this religion is closely associated with the spirit of freedom, social unrest, and rebellion against the powers that be. The colonizers at this time were deeply afraid of the effects of the unification that could be found in the practice of this religion. Rightfully so, because Voodoo became a tool to fuel resistance against oppression and finally secure the enslaved African peoples' freedom. Knowing this caused the colonialists to put all of their resources into making sure that this religion would be demonized to keep the enslaved people from dissenting or resisting their rule.

The erroneous assumptions of the ignorant about Voodoo are further fueled by how Hollywood represents it. Hollywood and popular culture have played a significant role in perpetuating negative stereotypes about Voodoo. In many movies and television shows, Voodoo is portrayed as a dark and mysterious practice associated with evil spirits, black magic, and human sacrifice. This depiction of Voodoo is often sensationalized and exaggerated; it does not accurately represent the true nature of the religion.

Another reason for the misrepresentation of Voodoo in popular culture is the influence of religious and cultural biases. Many Western societies have a history of demonizing non-Christian religions, particularly those practiced by enslaved or colonized peoples. In the case of Voodoo, this bias has led to the spread of false and negative beliefs about religion. Despite these misconceptions, Voodoo is a deeply spiritual and empowering religion emphasizing personal growth, community, and connection with the natural world. Its practices and beliefs are based on a deep reverence for ancestors, nature, and the divine. Its rituals and ceremonies are designed to connect practitioners with these powerful spiritual forces.

In recent years, there has been a growing interest in Voodoo as a legitimate spiritual practice. Efforts are being made to reclaim its rightful place as a powerful and transformative religion. Through education, cultural exchange, and greater representation in popular media, many practitioners are working to dispel the myths and misconceptions that have long plagued the religion and to celebrate its rich history and enduring legacy of revolution, freedom, and spiritual enlightenment.

Madame Laveau

Madame Laveau, the Voodoo Queen of New Orleans, was a powerful figure in Louisiana Voodoo. Her legacy is a testament to the enduring power of this spiritual tradition and the people who practice it. Born in 1801, Madame Laveau was a woman of remarkable strength and resilience. She rose to prominence in the early 19th century as a leader of the Voodoo community in New Orleans. Her knowledge of the rituals and practices of Voodoo was unparalleled, and her followers revered her for her ability to heal the sick and cast powerful spells.

This powerful woman's influence extended far beyond the Voodoo community. She was a respected figure in New Orleans society and was known for her acts of charity and kindness. She used her position of power to advocate for marginalized people's rights and fight against the injustices of the time. Madame Laveau's impact on Louisiana Voodoo was profound. She helped to shape the rituals and practices of the tradition, and her legacy continues to inspire Voodoo practitioners to this day. Her reputation as a powerful conjurer and healer has made her a legendary figure in the world of Voodoo, and her spirit is said to still be present in New Orleans. You could say that her life and legacy are a testament to the power of Voodoo and its ability to transform lives. She was a true pioneer and a visionary, and her contributions to the tradition will never be forgotten.

Dr. John

Dr. John, the Voodoo practitioner, was known for his deep roots in Louisiana Voodoo. He was a master of the mystical arts and a powerful practitioner of the rituals and spells that are at the heart of this complex spiritual tradition. Through his music, Dr. John brought the magic and mystery of Louisiana Voodoo to a wider audience. He infused his songs with the rhythms and incantations of the Voodoo ceremonies that he had witnessed and participated in throughout his life. He drew upon the spiritual traditions of his ancestors and the teachings of his mentors to create a unique and powerful expression that resonated with audiences worldwide.

Dr. John was a skilled practitioner of the Voodoo arts and was respected by the Voodoo community in New Orleans and beyond. He was known for performing powerful spells and healing the sick and suffering using herbs, oils, and other natural remedies. In addition to his musical and spiritual contributions, Dr. John was also a champion of the cultural heritage of Louisiana and its people. He was a tireless advocate for the preservation of the unique traditions and customs of the region, including Voodoo. He worked to ensure that they would be passed down to future generations.

This man's influence on Louisiana Voodoo and the broader cultural landscape of New Orleans cannot be overstated. He was a true visionary and a master of his craft, and his legacy will continue to inspire and guide people for generations to come. The doctor was a remarkable figure who wove the threads of the mystical and the music into a singular tapestry. He was born in New Orleans, Louisiana, in the early 20th century and grew up in the heart of the city's rich cultural gumbo. He came to be known as "Dr. John" after the Voodoo priest of the same name who lived in the 19th century. He was a master of the piano, a true bluesman who played with soul and passion. He infused his music with the rhythms of his beloved New Orleans, the African diaspora, and the sounds of the bayou.

Dr. John's music was not only a celebration of the rich cultural heritage of New Orleans but also a potent expression of the human experience. He sang of love, heartache, joy, and sorrow. He was a storyteller, a bard who wove tales of the people and places he knew so well. Dr. John's legacy lives on through his music and the many lives that he touched. He was a visionary, a pioneer, and a true original. His artistry was a testament to the power of the human spirit, and his life was a testament to the transformative power of music.

Chapter Two: Getting Ready for Voodoo

So, you want to serve the Loa, but there's a big question that's been bothering you. You're wondering if it's okay to just up and start Voodoo right away, head first, with no preparation. Well, the first thing you need to understand is if you truly want to practice this, you've got to be initiated.

Voodoo dolls.
https://www.flickr.com/photos/wcouch/3464210637

The Importance of Formal Initiation

The importance of initiation in Voodoo cannot be overstated. It is a sacred religion that demands deep respect and reverence. It cannot be taken lightly or approached without the proper guidance and training. In Voodoo, priests and priestesses are known respectively as houngans and mambos. These individuals have been initiated into the religion and have undergone a rigorous process of training and study. They hold a deep understanding of the practices and traditions of Voodoo and can guide practitioners through the initiation process.

To find true houngans and mambos, it is important to do your research and be cautious. Unfortunately, some try to scam individuals by pretending to be Voodoo practitioners. These individuals often make unrealistic promises or ask for large sums of money in exchange for their services. It is essential to be wary of such individuals and to seek out legitimate practitioners. One way to tell if a houngan or mambo is the real deal is to look for recommendations from other Voodoo community practitioners or members. You can also seek out individuals who have been practicing for many years and have a deep knowledge of the practices and traditions of the religion. A true houngan or mambo will also be respectful and cautious in their approach and will not promise unrealistic results.

The requirements for initiation into Voodoo can vary depending on the house or community. In general, however, it involves a process of training, study, and ritual. This can include learning about the history and traditions of the religion, developing a relationship with spirits and ancestors, and participating in ritual practices. It is a deeply personal and spiritual journey that requires dedication and commitment. By seeking out true houngans and mambos and undergoing the initiation process, you can develop a deep understanding and appreciation of the practices and traditions of Voodoo. Through this process, you can fully connect with the powerful forces of the universe and embrace the spiritual practices of religion.

The Role of the House

In the rich and vibrant tapestry of Louisiana Voodoo, practitioners are not simply lone individuals but are often part of a larger community called a "house." These houses are spiritual families that provide their members guidance, support, and protection. Practitioners are grouped into houses based on a shared spiritual lineage or tradition. Each house has its own unique practices, rituals, and beliefs, which have been passed down through generations of Voodoo practitioners. These houses often have a patriarch or matriarch, who is considered the spiritual leader and provides guidance to the members.

You stand to gain a lot when you're part of a house because it provides a sense of community and belonging and allows for deeper spiritual growth and development. Members of a house can learn from each other, share experiences, and support each other through the ups and downs of life. But being part of a house is not simply about socializing or having a sense of belonging. It is also a serious commitment to the practice of Voodoo. Houses are responsible for ensuring that their members follow correct protocol and conduct their spiritual work responsibly and respectfully. The role of a house is to provide a safe and supportive environment for its members to practice Voodoo and to guide them on their spiritual journeys. It is a place of learning and growth where practitioners can develop their abilities and gain a deeper understanding of the mysteries of the universe.

Becoming a Priestess or Priest

Voodoo is a way of life, a path to enlightenment, and a call to the divine. To answer the call of the spirits and become a houngan or mambo is not a decision to be taken lightly. It requires a deep commitment to faith, a willingness to learn, and a surrender to the mysteries of the universe. The path is not easy, but it is rewarding for those called to it. The process of becoming a houngan or mambo takes time and dedication. It is not something that can be rushed, nor can it be undertaken lightly. It requires a period of study, reflection, and contemplation under the guidance of an experienced priest or priestess.

Aspiring houngans and mambos must undergo a series of initiations, each one bringing them closer to the divine. These initiations are complex and highly ritualistic, with each step requiring the mastery of a new set of skills and knowledge. Through the initiations, the houngan or mambo becomes more deeply connected to the spirits and more capable of harnessing their power. The journey to becoming a houngan or mambo cannot be taken alone. It requires the support of a community, a house, of fellow practitioners who can guide and mentor the aspirant on their path. These houses are not just social clubs but deeply spiritual organizations, each with its own traditions, practices, and secrets.

The role of a house is to provide a home for the practitioner, a place to develop their skills, to learn from others, and to be supported on their journey. The benefits of being in a house are many, including access to resources, protection from negative energy, and guidance from experienced practitioners. Being called to become a houngan or mambo is not a decision that is made lightly. It is a calling from the spirits, a path to enlightenment, and a way of life. For those who are called to it, the journey is difficult, but it is also one of the most rewarding and fulfilling paths one can undertake.

Mental Preparation

The following are essential tips to help you mentally prepare to practice Voodoo.

Spend time in nature: Take time to connect with nature and observe its cycles. Pay attention to the plants, animals, and elements around you. Nature is an essential element of Louisiana Voodoo, a religion that is deeply connected to the natural world. Practitioners of Voodoo believe that all things in nature, from the trees to the animals, are filled with spiritual energy that can be harnessed and channeled for magical purposes. Time outside allows you to connect with this energy and develop a deeper understanding of the natural cycles central to Voodoo practice.

When you spend time in nature, you can learn to recognize the signs of the changing seasons, the phases of the moon, and the rhythms of the tides. You can observe the behavior of animals and birds and learn to read the messages they may be trying to convey. By immersing yourself in the natural world, you can begin to attune yourself to the flow of energy that connects all living things and develop a greater sense of harmony and balance in your life.

For a Voodoo practitioner, this connection to the natural world is essential, as it provides a foundation for their magical work. By learning to work with the energy of the natural world, practitioners of Voodoo can harness this energy to create positive change in their lives and in the lives of those around them. So, take time to connect with nature, observe its cycles, and learn its secrets. In doing so, you will be preparing yourself to enter into the rich and complex world of Louisiana Voodoo.

Practice mindfulness: Practice being present in the moment, observing your thoughts without judgment. By cultivating mindfulness, you can develop a deeper connection with the spirits and the natural world.

Meditation is a great way to develop this important skill – a crucial element of the spiritual journey, allowing you to observe your thoughts and become aware of your surroundings. Through meditation, you can quiet your mind and focus on your breath, allowing you to be fully present in every waking moment.

This awareness allows you to connect with the Loa and the energy around you, opening the way for deeper spiritual experiences.

The following are exercises you can do to raise your vibration and get you in the right space mentally and energetically to practice Voodoo:

Candle-gazing Meditation

1. Find a quiet place to sit and light a candle. Make sure there's nothing around it that could catch fire.
2. Begin to focus on the flame, letting your eyes become fixated on it.
3. Allow your breathing to become deep and slow, and try to keep your focus on the flame.
4. As thoughts arise, acknowledge them, then return your focus to the flame.
5. Try to stay in this meditative state for at least 5-10 minutes.

Loving-Kindness Meditation

1. Find a quiet and comfortable place to sit or lie down.
2. Start by focusing on your breath, taking deep breaths in through your nose and out through your slightly parted lips.
3. Once you've found a calm and centered state, focus on the people you care about in your life.
4. Envision sending them positive energy and love, picturing it as a bright light radiating from your heart center.
5. Expand the circle of people you're sending love to, including those you may have difficult relationships with or even people

you don't know well.

6. Finish the meditation by bringing the focus back to yourself, envisioning the same loving energy radiating from within you.

Read and study: Learn as much as possible about Voodoo's history, traditions, and practices. This can help you gain a deeper understanding and appreciation for the religion. To become a Voodooist, you must first immerse yourself in the rich history, traditions, and practices of the religion. Reading and studying can help you gain a deeper understanding and appreciation for Voodoo and provide a foundation for your own practice.

By learning about the origins and evolution of Voodoo, the beliefs and customs, the symbolism and rituals, you can begin to see the beauty and complexity of this ancient religion. Studying Voodoo can also help you understand the roles and responsibilities of a practitioner and how to approach the Loa with respect and humility. By reading about the experiences of other Voodoo practitioners, you can gain insight into the challenges and rewards of this path and learn from the wisdom of those who have gone before you. Remember, knowledge is power, and by arming yourself with knowledge about Voodoo, you can prepare yourself mentally and spiritually for the practice. With an open mind and a willing spirit, you can learn and grow in the ways of the Loa.

Connect with your ancestors: Honor your ancestors and learn about your family history. This can help you feel more grounded and connected to your roots. Connecting with your ancestors is crucial in preparing yourself to practice Voodoo. Ancestral veneration is an integral part of Voodoo, and the religion emphasizes maintaining a strong connection with one's lineage. By learning about your family history and honoring your ancestors, you gain a deeper understanding of your personal history and tap into the spiritual power believed to flow from one's ancestors. In Voodoo, the spirits of the dead are believed to profoundly influence the living. Practitioners who neglect to connect with their ancestors risk being cut off from this source of spiritual power. By tending to and improving relationships with your ancestors, you establish a foundation of respect and reverence that can help you navigate the complex spiritual landscape of Voodoo with grace and sensitivity.

Cultivate intuition: Practice trusting your gut instincts and intuition. You can start by paying attention to your body and noticing how it responds to different situations. Fostering your intuition is a critical component of preparing for the practice of Voodoo. Voodoo is a religion that values intuition, instinct, and spiritual discernment. When you learn to trust your intuition, you are more in tune with the energy and spirit around you. This awareness can help in your interactions with the Loa, your ancestors, and the world around you. By paying attention to your body, you can begin to recognize the signs and signals it gives you. Your gut instincts may alert you to situations that feel off or dangerous or guide you toward people and experiences that will be positive and uplifting. This practice of listening to your body and intuition can help you develop a deeper sense of trust in yourself and your instincts, which can be very beneficial in the practice of Voodoo.

In Voodoo, the Loa is believed to communicate with you through your intuition and spiritual senses. By developing your intuition, you may be better able to discern the messages and guidance the Loa send you. By strengthening your intuition and practicing spiritual discernment, you will be better equipped to navigate the Voodoo world and connect with its energies and entities.

The following are exercises that will help you with your intuition:

Body Scan Exercise

1. Find a quiet place to sit or lie down and close your eyes.
2. Take a few deep breaths and allow your body to relax. Breathe in through your nostrils and out through your slightly parted lips.
3. Starting at the top of your head, focus on each part of your body, one at a time, slowly moving down to your toes.
4. Notice any sensations, tension, or discomfort you feel in each area and observe them without judgment.
5. Allow yourself to feel any emotions or memories that may come up during the scan.
6. Now, allow that part of your body to relax. You can imagine it's made of cement, and it sinks deeper and deeper into relaxation, heavier with each breath.
7. After completing the scan, take a few deep breaths and slowly open your eyes.

Intuitive Journaling

1. Set aside time each day to sit and write in a journal.
2. Start by asking yourself a question or setting an intention for the session.
3. Write down any thoughts or feelings that come to mind without judgment or analysis.
4. Pay attention to any recurring themes or patterns in your writing.
5. After finishing your writing, take a few deep breaths and reflect on what you wrote.

Intuitive Decision-making

1. When faced with a decision, take a moment to pause and take a few deep breaths.
2. Tune in to your body and notice any physical sensations that arise.
3. Ask yourself how each option makes you feel, both emotionally and physically.
4. Pay attention to any intuitive nudges or insights that come up.
5. Make a decision based on what feels most aligned with your intuition rather than overthinking or analyzing.

You must understand that intuition is like a muscle. "Use it or lose it." You need to give it time to get stronger, and you must be consistent with the exercises to get better at reading your gut.

Recommended Reading

There are many books you could read to help you along your journey. Here is a list of five of the best ones available:

- *"Mama Lola: A Vodou Priestess in Brooklyn"* by Karen McCarthy Brown — This book is a personal account of the life and practice of a Haitian Vodou priestess, Mama Lola, who has been practicing for over 40 years. It provides an in-depth look at the day-to-day activities of a Vodou practitioner and includes an exploration of the religion's history, traditions, and beliefs.

- *"The New Orleans Voodoo Handbook"* by Kenaz Filan — This book includes information on the history, beliefs, and practices of Louisiana Voodoo.

- *"Voodoo in New Orleans"* by Robert Tallant — This book explores the history of Voodoo in New Orleans and includes information on the practice of Louisiana Voodoo.

- *"The Magic of Marie Laveau: Embracing the Spiritual Legacy of the Voodoo Queen of New Orleans"* by Denise Alvarado — This book is a comprehensive guide to the practice of Louisiana Voodoo and includes information on the life and legacy of the famous Voodoo queen, Marie Laveau.

- *"The Rootworker's Guide to Healing and Wellness"* by Stephanie Rose Bird — This book includes information on the practice of rootwork, which is closely related to Louisiana Voodoo, and provides guidance on how to use herbs, roots, and other natural remedies for healing.

Please note that these recommendations are just a starting point and that many other books are available on Voodoo. As always, it is important to approach any new spiritual practice with an open mind and a spirit of inquiry and to do your own research to find the most helpful resources. You should educate yourself because Voodoo is a sacred religion. You can't just jump into it or do rituals just because you feel like it! Resist the temptation to play things by ear, and please don't just fool around with invoking spirits; instead, do the right thing by seeking to be formally initiated and respect this way of life.

If you want to learn more about how important spirits and ancestors are to the practice of Louisiana Voodoo and you're curious about how to energetically cleanse your home and keep it protected and safe, you're definitely going to want to keep reading.

Chapter Three: Ingredients and Materials You Might Need

The materials used in Voodoo spells are not merely physical ingredients but rather bear great spiritual significance. The practitioner needs to understand the significance of these materials and the roles they play in Voodoo rituals. Each material carries its own unique energy and spiritual symbolism, and the proper understanding of these elements is necessary for the successful practice of Louisiana Voodoo.

Herbs and roots, candles, and oils are the three primary materials used in Voodoo spells; each carries its own spiritual significance. Only by taking the time to understand the spiritual meanings of these materials can one properly harness their power and incorporate them into their rituals. By studying the meanings and uses of these materials, one can learn to create their own spells that align with their unique needs and intentions. Understanding the materials and their spiritual meanings is crucial for the successful practice of Louisiana Voodoo and for cultivating a deeper understanding of the religion as a whole.

Herbs and Roots

Herbs and roots play a vital role in Louisiana Voodoo. They are used in spells to harness the power of nature and work in tandem with the universe's energies. Regarding Voodoo, every plant and root has its own spiritual meaning, role, and usage in spells. One of the most essential aspects of working with herbs and roots in Voodoo is understanding their properties and their energies. It is said that every herb and root has its unique vibration, and when used in spells, it can help enhance the desired outcome. The following is a list of 59 herbs and roots, along with their spiritual meanings, roles, and usage in spells:

Herbs and roots are essential to voodoo practices.
https://unsplash.com/photos/iSGbjKZ9erg

1. Angelica Root: used for protection, uncrossing, and luck in gambling spells.
2. Bay Leaf: used for protection and purification.
3. Black Cohosh: used for protection and cleansing.
4. Black Salt: used for protection and banishing.
5. Bladderwrack: used for protection and enhancing psychic powers.
6. Blessed Thistle: used for protection and purification.
7. Blue Cohosh: used for protection and enhancing psychic powers.
8. Boneset: used for protection and healing.
9. Calamus Root: used for commanding and controlling spells.
10. Camphor: used for purification and protection.
11. Catnip: used for love and luck spells.
12. Cedar: used for purification and protection.
13. Cinnamon: used for success, protection, and money spells.
14. Clove: used for protection and banishing spells.

15. Comfrey: used for protection and healing spells.

16. Copal: used for purification and cleansing.

17. Damiana: used for love and lust spells.

18. Dandelion: used for divination and calling spirits.

19. Devil's Shoestring: used for protection and luck spells.

20. Dragon's Blood: used for protection and purification.

21. Eucalyptus: used for healing and purification.

22. Fennel: Used for purification and protection.

23. Frankincense: used for purification and cleansing.

24. Five Finger Grass: used for attracting success and opportunities.

25. Galangal: used for uncrossing and protection.

26. Ginger: used for love and money spells.

27. Hawthorn: used for protection and banishing spells.

28. Hyssop: used for purification and protection.

29. Jasmine: used for love and psychic enhancement.

30. Juniper: used for protection and banishing spells.

31. Kava Kava: used for protection and psychic enhancement.

32. Lavender: used for love, purification, and healing.

33. Lemon Balm: used for love and happiness spells.

34. Lemon Grass: used for psychic enhancement and purification.

35. Licorice Root: used for commanding and controlling spells.

36. Lucky Hand Root: used for good luck.

37. Mandrake Root: used for protection and increasing personal power.

38. Mugwort: used for divination and enhancing psychic powers.

39. Mullein: used for protection and banishing spells.

40. Myrrh: used for purification and protection.

41. Nettle: used for protection and uncrossing spells.

42. Olive: used for protection and peace spells.

43. Orange Peel: used for love spells.

44. Patchouli: used for love and money spells.

45. Peppermint: used for purification and healing.

46. Pine: used for purification and protection.

47. Red Clover: used for love and money spells.

48. Rose: used for love and protection.

49. Rue: used for protection and uncrossing spells.

50. Sage: used for purification and protection.

51. Sandalwood: used for purification and protection.

52. Sweetgrass: used for purification.

53. Wormwood: spiritual grounding, protection, psychic abilities, divination

54. Yarrow: courage, love, psychic abilities, protection, exorcism

55. Yellow Dock: healing, money, fertility, attraction, success

56. Yerba Santa: purification, protection, spiritual growth, psychic abilities.

57. Ylang Ylang: love, romance, sensuality, calming, relaxation.

58. Zedoary: money, luck, protection, divination, love.

59. Zinnia: love, friendship, abundance, courage, happiness.

Candles

Candles play a vital role in Voodoo spells, as they are used to focus and direct energy towards a specific goal or intention. Different colors of candles have different meanings and are associated with specific purposes. In Voodoo, the color of the candle used in a spell is often chosen based on the desired outcome or intention of the practitioner. When choosing a candle for a spell, it is important to consider its color, size, and shape. Some practitioners prefer to use plain, unscented candles. In contrast, others prefer scented candles with specific aromas corresponding to the intention of the spell.

Different candles of varying colors symbolize intentions in voodoo rituals.
https://unsplash.com/photos/iSyyY1GfYSw

Now let's talk about candle colors. The use of colors in Voodoo is based on the belief that each color represents a specific energy or intention. The origins of this practice are not entirely clear, as it is a part of the oral tradition passed down through generations of practitioners. However, it is believed that the use of colors in Voodoo can be traced back to West African spiritual practices. In Voodoo, each color is associated with certain attributes and energies. For example, red is often associated with passion, love, and courage, while black is associated with protection and banishing negative energies. Green is often associated with money, abundance, and prosperity, while white is associated with purity, peace, and healing.

The practice of using colors in Voodoo spells and rituals is based on the idea that like attracts like. By using candles, fabrics, or other materials of a certain color, practitioners can draw in the energy or intention associated with that color. For example, if someone wanted to attract love, they might use a red candle to represent the passion and energy of love. Remember that when you use colors in Voodoo, you're enhancing and directing the energy of your spell or ritual. Practitioners can create a powerful and effective spell or ritual by choosing the right color and understanding its associated energies and intentions. You can also blend colors, depending on what it is you want to accomplish. Here is a list of recommended candles and their spiritual meanings, roles, and usage in spells:

1. Red candle: used in love spells, passion spells, strength spells, and courage spells.
2. Pink candle: used in friendship spells, romance spells, and emotional healing spells.
3. Orange candle: used in creativity spells, success spells, and confidence spells.
4. Yellow candle: used in communication spells, clarity spells, and inspiration spells.
5. Green candle: used in fertility spells, growth spells, abundance spells, and financial success spells.
6. Blue candle: used in healing spells, peace spells, and tranquility spells
7. Purple candle: used in psychic ability spells, spirituality spells, and transformation spells.

8. White candle: used in purification spells, protection spells, and spiritual enlightenment spells.

9. Black candle: used in banishing negativity spells, breaking hexes spells, and protection spells.

When using candles in Voodoo spells, it is important to light them with intention, focusing your energy and attention on the desired outcome. Some practitioners prefer to anoint their candles with oils, carve symbols or words into them, or use them in conjunction with other materials such as crystals, herbs, or talismans to enhance the effectiveness of the spell.

Special Candles

Other kinds of special candles are used in Voodoo beyond traditional taper candles. Here are a few examples:

1. **Seven-day candles:** These are larger candles that are meant to burn continuously for seven days. They are often used in longer spells or rituals and can be inscribed with specific symbols or words.

2. **Figure candles:** These candles are shaped like people or animals and can be used to represent a specific individual or to draw upon the spiritual qualities of that person or animal. For example, a black cat candle could be used for protection or luck, while a red human-shaped candle could be used for love spells.

3. **Reversible candles:** These are candles that are black on one end and red on the other and are used in spells to reverse negativity or harm back onto the person who sent it.

4. **Double-action candles:** These are candles that have two colors, typically black on one end and another color (such as green or red) on the other. They are used to both remove negative energy and bring in positive energy.

5. **Jumbo candles:** These are large candles that come in a variety of shapes and colors. They can be used in place of multiple candles or to create a stronger, more intense flame.

6. **Skull candles:** These are molded in the shape of a human skull. They are used in spells related to communication with the dead and for spells related to mental powers and influencing others.

7. **Black cat candles:** These are candles shaped like a black cat. They are used in spells related to luck, protection, and even for breaking curses or hexes.

8. **Devil candles:** These are molded in the shape of a devil or a demon. They are used in spells related to banishing negative energies or entities.

Oils

The use of oils in New Orleans Voodoo is based on the belief that they possess spiritual and magical properties that can be harnessed to influence specific aspects of life. The roots of this practice can be traced back to the early African spiritual practices which formed the foundation of Voodoo. Many plants and herbs have been used for centuries for their medicinal and magical properties, and the essential oils extracted from these plants are believed to have similar properties.

In New Orleans Voodoo, oils are often used as part of spellwork, an important aspect of the tradition. Each oil is believed to have a specific spiritual meaning and can be used for various purposes, from attracting love and wealth to protection and banishing negative energies. When used with candles, herbs, and other ritual tools, oils are believed to enhance the spell's effectiveness.

The exact origins of the use of oils in Voodoo are unclear, but it is believed to have been a common practice among many African and Afro-Caribbean spiritual traditions. Some believe that the use of oils may have been influenced by ancient Egyptian and other Middle Eastern cultures, which also used essential oils in religious ceremonies and as part of healing practices. Oils are absolutely important when it comes to spellwork. You see, oils are used in many different ways in the practice of Voodoo, from anointing candles and other objects to dressing oneself for a ritual. Each oil has its own unique spiritual meaning, role, and usage in spells, and knowing which oil to use for a particular purpose is key to success in Voodoo. Now, here are 54 of the recommended oils in Louisiana Voodoo, along with their spiritual meanings, roles, and usage in spells:

- Almond oil: prosperity, fertility, and wisdom
- Basil oil: purification, protection, and prosperity
- Bayberry oil: prosperity, success, and protection

- Bay leaf oil: protection, purification, and psychic abilities
- Benzoin oil: purification, protection, and prosperity
- Bergamot oil: money, success, and mental clarity
- Black pepper oil: protection, purification, and energy
- Camphor oil: purification and protection
- Caraway oil: protection, purification, and mental clarity
- Cardamom oil: love, sensuality, and mental clarity
- Cedarwood oil: purification, protection, and healing
- Chamomile oil: relaxation, purification, and psychic abilities
- Cinnamon oil: love, success, and power
- Citronella oil: repelling negative energy and insects
- Clove oil: protection, love, and wealth
- Coconut oil: purification and protection
- Cypress oil: protection, purification, and healing
- Dragon's Blood oil: protection and banishing negative energy
- Eucalyptus oil: healing, purification, and protection
- Frankincense oil: spiritual purification, protection, and healing
- Gardenia oil: love, peace, and protection
- Fennel oil: purification, protection, and prosperity
- Geranium oil: love, sensuality, and psychic abilities
- Ginger oil: love and prosperity
- Grapefruit oil: energy and protection
- Jasmine oil: love, spiritual growth, and psychic abilities
- Juniper oil: protection, purification, and healing
- Lavender oil: relaxation, peace, and healing
- Lemon oil: purification, protection, and love
- Lemongrass oil: purification, protection, and psychic abilities
- Lime oil: purification, love, and healing
- Lotus oil: spiritual growth, enlightenment, and purity
- Magnolia oil: love, attraction, and purity

- Mint oil: healing, purification, and prosperity
- Musk oil: sensuality, attraction, and grounding
- Myrrh oil: purification, protection, and healing
- Neroli oil: love, relaxation, and purification
- Nutmeg oil: luck, prosperity, and clarity
- Orange oil: love, purification, and energy
- Orris root oil: divination, psychic abilities, and protection
- Patchouli oil: love, prosperity, and grounding
- Peppermint oil: purification, protection, and mental clarity
- Pine oil: purification, protection, and healing
- Rose oil: love, beauty, and psychic abilities
- Rosemary oil: protection, purification, and mental clarity
- Sandalwood oil: purification, protection, and healing
- Spearmint oil: healing, purification, and protection
- Sweetgrass oil: purification, protection, and spiritual growth
- Tea tree oil: purification, protection, and healing
- Thyme oil: courage, purification, and protection
- Vanilla oil: love, sensuality, and passion
- Vetiver oil: grounding, protection, and sensuality
- Yarrow oil: protection, healing, and psychic abilities
- Ylang-ylang oil: love, sensuality, and relaxation

Safety Matters!

It is of utmost importance to note that some of the herbs and oils used in Voodoo practices can be quite dangerous if ingested or used improperly. Anyone wishing to engage in such practices must do so cautiously and carefully. For example, the ingestion of certain herbs can lead to serious health issues; even contact with certain oils can result in skin irritation or allergic reactions. Additionally, ensuring that any items used in Voodoo spells do not harm the environment is vital. So, once more, when it comes to using herbs and oils in Voodoo practices, you must exercise great care, respect, and responsibility.

It is important to note that pregnant women should be cautious when using any type of oil, especially during the first trimester. Oils that should be avoided during pregnancy include basil, birch, camphor, cinnamon, clary sage, clove, fennel, hyssop, juniper, marjoram, myrrh, peppermint, rosemary, sage, and thyme. Some oils are more likely to cause allergic reactions than others. These include cinnamon, clove, lemongrass, and tea tree oils. It is always recommended to perform a patch test before using any new oil or product on the skin.

Individuals with certain medical conditions should avoid using certain oils. For example, those with high blood pressure should avoid using stimulating oils such as rosemary and peppermint, while individuals with epilepsy should avoid using stimulating oils such as rosemary, peppermint, and eucalyptus. People with asthma should avoid using oils that may trigger an attack, such as eucalyptus and peppermint.

It is also important to note that some oils can be toxic to animals and plants. Oils such as tea tree, cinnamon, and citrus oils can be toxic to cats and dogs. When using oils around pets, it is important to use them in a well-ventilated area and ensure that pets cannot ingest or come into contact with them. Additionally, some oils can be harmful to plants. For example, peppermint oil can be toxic to certain plants and may even kill them. When using oils around plants, it is important to research their effects beforehand and to use caution when applying oils near plants.

Now, you're probably dying to get to know more about the Creator and his helper spirits. In the next chapter, you'll get all your burning questions answered and then some.

Chapter Four: Bondye and the Loa Pantheon

You cannot claim to practice Voodoo without knowing everything there is to know about Bondye, or the Supreme Creator, as well as the Loa (or Lwa). These are the most important aspects of Voodoo.

Bondye is the supreme creator of the universe.
https://pixabay.com/es/illustrations/meditaci%C3%B3n-reflexi%C3%B3n-universo-5286678/

Voodoo Gods, Catholic Saints

From 1501, Africans were enslaved and taken to the Caribbean colonies to be put to work on sugar plantations and mines. It would remain so until 1821 – when Spain would finally declare the slave trade illegal. By 1860, there were about 350,000 enslaved people in Cuba. These people comprised many Yoruba people from Nigeria, and they were from Ijebu, Ife, Kesu, and Egba, among other Yoruba regions. Now, you can find these same people in Togo and Benin, too. The Yorubas who arrived were natural farmers. Their culture had a societal structure made up of different kingdoms.

One thing to note about Yoruba culture is that it has a very rich mythology. Take the Yoruba pantheon, for instance. It's a rather broad one, made up of divine beings. Each one is known as an Orisa (pronounced o-ri-sha). Sometimes, the word is spelled "Orisha." Among them are Sango (pronounced shaw-ngo), Oyo (pronounced aw-yaw), Yemoja, Egba, Obatala, Ogun, etc. These beings are the ones who keep the Yoruba people safe. When the enslaved Africans were coerced into leaving their lands for Brazil, Haiti, Cuba, and Santo Domingo, they had to find creative ways to continue to practice their religion. This led to Voodoo's syncretism with Roman Catholicism, the latter being the religion of the colonial masters.

Syncretism is simply the process of combining different religious views or ideologies to fit each other. It's about merging different practices, theologically speaking, so that there's some form of unity, making it possible for one to practice different religions without dealing with the cognitive dissonance that inevitably arises from trying to follow two distinctly different ways of life. So, there was a blend of Voodoo with Roman Catholicism. You can also find elements of Freemasonry as well.

The Black Codes, also known as the Code Noir, were implemented during the French and Spanish colonization of New Orleans. This was in 1724. The codes were meant to cover all things related to the enslaved people's affairs. The code also stipulated that they were not permitted to practice their religions out in the open. It also stipulated that all enslavers had to convert the enslaved people to Christianity no later than eight days after they got to the colony. They were to be taught Roman Catholic beliefs and had to be baptized as well. So as the enslaved people were taught about Catholicism, they found ways to incorporate their traditional African beliefs with what they were learning.

Sometimes, the enslavers were a little "kinder" because of the festivities of holidays like Easter and Christmas. They would let the enslaved people have liberty, if only for a while. The people were still colonized but would be allowed some time off to spend the holidays as they liked. They also had some free time on Sunday afternoons. The enslaved people took advantage of their freedom — which should have been rightfully theirs anyway — to practice their religions with others. Sunday afternoons, they would all meet up in Congo Square, an area designated by the rules in New Orleans for the African people to get together. There, they would create their own customs and traditions.

The people found a way to connect their deities or Loa with the Roman Catholic saints. For instance, in Saint Peter, they saw Papa Legba since he is known as the one who unlocks the spirit realm to grant access to it, and Saint Peter is usually painted or drawn with keys in hand. In the Mater Dolorosa, they found Ezili Freda, a Loa who loves everything to do with luxury and love. In Saint Patrick, the Voodooists found Damballa, a snake. The saint is usually shown with snakes. Sometimes they consider Damballa to be Moses since he was the one whose staff became a snake that swallowed all the other snakes of the Egyptian priests when God sent him to free the Israelites. Cosmos and Damian were originally physicians of Arab origin, twin brothers who would eventually become Christian martyrs. In them, the Africans saw the Marasa, who are sacred twin Loas.

Bondye

Voodoo is a practice centered on the belief in a creator known as Bondye. Etymologically, the name Bondye is from the French Bon Dieu, meaning "Good God." This is the uncreated Creator who is in charge of all things. Some refer to this creator as Gran Met, meaning the Great Master. In terms of ideology, this God is almost the same as the Christian concept of God. However, when it comes to Voodoo, no one is to approach Bondye directly because that would be disrespectful and an exercise in futility.

The way to approach Bondye is through the Lwa (or Loa), who represent the different expressions of the Creator's power. Approaching Bondye directly is pointless because this being is beyond your comprehension since you're human, and he's so much more. So, the only way to get through to him and receive from him is through the Loa.

This is why Voodooists turn their attention to these beings instead and why you'll never hear anyone claim that Bondye himself has possessed them. Does this mean Bondye doesn't care about human affairs? Of course not. You must understand that everything is part of Bondye's plan — even when it doesn't seem that way.

Every Voodooist knows that there's not a single person or thing that isn't connected to the Gran Met. Therefore, Bondye must be acknowledged and honored using the correct methods and rites at all ceremonies. This being is shrouded in mystery and is beyond human comprehension. He is the Unknowable who knows all, the one who keeps the wheel of life spinning in perpetuity. Some people may erroneously assume that because Bondye is literally the "Good God," there is some equal and opposing force that one might call "Mal Dieu" or the "Bad God." That is not the case at all.

Naturally, this would cause some confusion for those who are used to assuming that all things in religion require duality. And this should, also naturally, cause you to wonder what the concepts of good and bad are in Bondye's eyes and in the eyes of the true Voodooist. The thing to understand is that it's not about good and bad but about the extent of the demonstration of Bondye's presence in your life. This demonstration comes down to the choices you make. So, doing things that bode well for you financially, physically, and in any other aspect of life is a good thing. When you do things that take away from that well-being, this would be considered as bad.

There's not a single person not made in the image of Bondye. There's nothing and no one who doesn't have Bondye's essence flowing through them. He crafted humanity using only clay and water, working with the very elements he used to create the world. Voodooists understand that they come from the earth and that it's no coincidence that when humans pass away, they return to the earth. Since all people are made of the same stuff that the earth is, it is a deeply rooted belief in Voodoo that there's not a thing that can work against you, even when it seems that way, since humans are all made of the same stuff.

The Loa Pantheon

The Loa or Lwa are divided into various pantheons, also known as nanchons (meaning "nations") or families. Each of these has its own requirements, methodologies, and ethos regarding rites and ceremonies.

It is said there are at least seventeen nanchons, but they're not all very popular or known, and some of them have been assimilated into the major ones. For instance, pantheons like the Wangol and Nago, also known as the Ibo and Kongo, are now a part of the Petro pantheon. The major pantheons are:

1. The Rada Loa
2. The Petro Loa
3. The Gede Loa

You may have heard someone claim that the Petro Loa are bad and that the Rada are the good guys. That person is sadly misinformed. Regarding the Loa, you cannot apply regular ethics to them and their magic. To be clear, there was once a period when the Petro was viewed as being connected to evil magic only, while the Rada was deemed as good. This led to the misconception that the Petro Loa are dangerous destroyers best left alone and that the Rada are very forgiving and lenient.

The truth of the matter is that Petro is capable of goodness and has demonstrated this time and time again. Also, as peaceful and sweet as the Rada Loa are, their revenge can be swift and ruthless if you cross them. You could ask devotees who fail to perform their religious obligations, and they'll tell you as much. So, avoid the trap of using basic ideas of morality to define the Loa pantheons. This doesn't mean you should assume Voodoo is a way of life free from morality and that you now have the license to be a terrible person. As a Voodooist, you are clear about right and wrong, and you also understand that, at the end of the day, it's all about your service to the Loa and ultimately to Bondye, who is the one who maintains the world as you know it.

The Rada Loa Pantheon

The etymological root of Rada is Arada, a Dahomien kingdom that existed during the colonization of Haiti. The Rada Loa are sometimes called the Gentle Ones because they're cool-headed and sweet. Before taking any action, they must carefully consider all the facts of the situation. For this reason, you can be sure that the judgment they deliver is just and deserved. They are particular about maintaining balance and harmony in all things.

The great thing about the Rada pantheon is that you can always depend on them. They love to be as connected to their loyal followers as possible, and they love the idea of family. You can tell from their names how much familial connections mean to them. All the rituals involved in the adoration of these Loa come from the Arada kingdom. One of the peculiar things about these beings is that their color is white, so it's not unusual to notice white cloths and other white things on altars dedicated to them. Some of the Rada Loa include, but aren't limited to:

- Papa Legba, who keeps the door and the gate.
- Ounto, the Loa of the drums.
- Marassa, the divine twins.
- Damballa Wedo, the spirit of peace and tranquility, and the Serpent Father
- Sobo, who brings prosperity
- La Sirene, the seductress who rules the sea
- Granne Halouba, the wise woman
- Erzilie Freda, the sweet Queen of beauty, luxury, and wealth.
- Bossou, the powerful bull
- Klemezin, the one who brings enlightenment
- Lovana, the one who removes obstacles

The Petro Loa Pantheon

The word "Petro" is said to come from Dom Pedro, the one who was at the helm of the 18th-century maroon rebellion. The spirits in this pantheon can also be collectively referred to as compete. These are the hot-headed spirits, and their ways are rather volatile. Everything about them is aggressive, but this is not necessarily bad. There is such a thing as positive aggression, you know. When they take action, there's an undeniable force about them. Regarding altars, it's best to have theirs separate from the Rada Loa's in the ounfo (meaning "temple"). You should also never invoke them at the same time as you invoke the Rada during your rituals and ceremonial rites.

Every Voodooist knows that the Petro Loa always come through dramatically, and for some reason, they're particularly good at making things happen regarding money. If you'll offer the Petro Loa anything, be prepared to give them coffee, hot peppers, alcohol, cigarettes, blood, and other things of that nature. If you ever witness a ceremony or ritual for these beings, you'll notice that the drumming is at a really rapid pace and feels very powerful, sometimes harsh. You'll see Voodooists with whips that they crack. Some blow whistles pretty loudly, and there's also exploding gunpowder. These Loa have red as their color, and in light of everything you've just read about them, it only makes sense. Some of the Petro Loa include but aren't limited to the following:

- Kalfou, the crossroads spirit
- Simbi Andeazo, the spirit of saltwater and freshwater, of the rain, and of baths
- Ti Jean Petro, the spirit of fire and revolution
- Gran Bwa, the tree spirit, the one who rules the night forest
- Simitye, he who brings change, the connection between Petro and Gede
- Ezili Danto, mother of Haiti
- Linglinsou, a violent spirit of vengeance

The Gede Loa Pantheon

Sometimes, Gede is spelled Ghede or Guede. These Loa are in charge of all matters concerning death and fertility. Their musical drumming and dancing style is known as Banda. Like the other Loa, they can and do possess the Voodooists around. When they do, they'll typically douse themselves in a mixture of 21 Scotch bonnet peppers and a raw sugarcane rum known as clairin. Sometimes they use goat peppers instead.

The Gede Loa is usually celebrated during a festival known as the Fet Gede, which happens on November 2nd each year. This is like All Souls' Day or the Festival of the Dead. Those who are devoted to these Loa will enjoy their generosity. If any good has been done for the people that has not been appreciated, they know that the Loa will avenge their lack of appreciation. These beings are very sensual. If you're not already familiar with their ways, you may find yourself appalled, but there's no reason to be. Irreverent beings, their dancing is a mimicry of sex. They're known for taking the dead to the next stage of life. The color of this pantheon is black. These are some of the Gede Loa:

- Papa Gede, the psychopomp
- Brav Gede, he who watches the graveyard
- Guede Nibo, the psychopomp and patron of those who passed on unnaturally
- Maman Brigitte, protector of gravestones
- Baron Criminel, the enforcer and first murderer

We'll look further into each pantheon in subsequent chapters, but for now, if you'd like to learn more about the Loa, you can always do some research.

Veves

In Voodoo, the devotees of Loas will occasionally ask the Loa to come and take over their bodies so that through them, they may communicate with others and interact with them. This isn't something that's just done anywhere, anytime. There are rituals with specific practices that must be followed to the letter. During rituals, you can expect to witness dancing, drumming, chanting, and other displays, especially when the possession has happened. During these rituals, veves become vital. These are special symbols that are connected to individual Loa. In the same way, every Loa has special dances, drum rhythms, colors, and so on, and they also have unique symbols that carry their energy. Usually, the veves are drawn on the sandy floor of the ritual space or on any powdery substance on the floor.

As the rituals carry on, the veves will serve as a platform of sorts where devotees can place their offerings to the Loa. It is important that the offerings made are energetically in resonance with the veves and the Loa that the devotees intend to invoke. Once the veve is drawn, libations are poured on it, and a candle is set in its center. To infuse life and energy into the veve, a devotee must ring a bell as everyone prays to the Loa. If there is ever a need to summon more than one Loa, all their veves must be drawn and linked, and special attention is given to the sort of powdery substance used for each of the Loa. Some like coffee powder, others prefer brick powder, and others prefer white powder.

While every Loa's veve is different (and with some Loa having more than one veve), some things remain constant with all of them. The veve acts as a lighthouse to draw all relevant ships to it. It is meant to draw the attention of the Loa, and not only that, but it also acts as an amplifier of the Loa's energy in that space. You may assume, therefore, that tattooing yourself with a Loa's veve would be just the thing to do to keep their presence with you always, or that you can just put it up wherever you want to in your home without much thought, but that's not the case.

Please don't tattoo yourself with a veve. The odds are, the Loa may choose to ignore you when you need them — and that's the best-case scenario. The worst thing that could happen due to you disrespecting the veves like that is you may upset the Petro spirits, and you already know that you don't want to be on their bad side. When using a veve, your intent must be clear and sincere. Again, Voodoo is a way of life, not an "aesthetic" to be shown off. Please treat it accordingly.

Now, it's time to look at some of the powerful female Loa of Louisiana Voodoo.

Chapter Five: Major Female Loa

This chapter takes a look at the most important Loa of Louisiana Voodoo, who are females. To be clear, this chapter doesn't cover every single female Loa in existence, so you may want to do further research if you would like to learn about any that aren't mentioned here.

Maman Brigitte

Maman Brigitte is the Loa of death and cemeteries in Louisiana Voodoo. She is a fiery and powerful force to be reckoned with and has a personality reflecting her association with death and the afterlife.

Maman Brigitte is the Loa of death.
https://www.pexels.com/photo/black-gold-14704594/

In appearance, Maman Brigitte is often depicted as a tall, statuesque woman with dark skin and fiery red hair. She is said to be regal and fierce, with piercing eyes that can see into the souls of those who cross her path.

Her veve is a powerful symbol, featuring a heart above a triangle and other intricate lines and patterns. Other symbols include a skull, crossbones, snake, and coffin. These symbols represent her connection to death and the afterlife and her role as a powerful healer and protector.

Maman Brigitte is often syncretized with the Roman Catholic saint, St. Brigid, known for her healing powers and association with fire and light.

In terms of her correspondences, Maman Brigitte is associated with the color purple and hot peppers, rum, and tobacco. She is said to be particularly fond of the herb rue, which is used in many Voodoo rituals and spells.

Maman Brigitte is closely associated with the Gede family of Loa, known for their irreverent and bawdy personalities. She is said to have a close relationship with Baron Samedi, the Loa of death and resurrection. She is often called upon to help guide souls to the afterlife.

Bits of lore connected to Maman Brigitte often depict her as a strong-willed, fearless woman unafraid of death or the unknown. She is said to have a fierce temper and a no-nonsense attitude but also a deep compassion for those seeking her guidance.

Preferred offerings for Maman Brigitte include rum, hot peppers, tobacco, and items associated with death and the afterlife, such as black candles and images of skulls or cemeteries. Signs that she has received and accepted one's offering may include a feeling of warmth or a sudden change in the atmosphere.

Maman Brigitte is celebrated and honored in New Orleans during the annual Day of the Dead festival and other Voodoo ceremonies throughout the year. She is often called upon to help guide souls to the afterlife and to offer protection to those who seek her aid.

Ezili Freda

In the world of Voodoo, there is a Loa known for her beauty, her elegance, and her love for all things luxurious. This is Ezili Freda, the Loa of love, sensuality, and luxury. Ezili Freda is often depicted as a light-skinned, beautiful woman dressed in a flowing white gown and adorned with pearls and other fine jewelry. Her veve, or sacred symbol, is a heart-shaped design that is often drawn in pink, white, and blue powders. She is syncretized with the Catholic saints Our Lady of Lourdes and the Immaculate Conception.

Ezili Freda.
https://www.wallpaperflare.com/woman-female-girl-white-dress-wood-forest-sleep-walking-wallpaper-aotmf

As the Loa of love and sensuality, Ezili Freda is associated with pink, white, and gold. She is often offered champagne, pink roses, and sweets such as white cake, sugar, and honey. In terms of plants and herbs, she is associated with jasmine, ylang-ylang, and vanilla. Ezili Freda is known to be a very powerful and respected Loa in the Voodoo pantheon. She is often seen as a mother figure and is revered for her ability to bring people together in love and harmony. Her relationships with other Loa are complex, but she is often associated with her counterpart, the Loa of war and struggle, Ogou, who is her protector and champion.

This Loa has connections to other spirits that run deep. Her nature as a love goddess means that she has ties to other spirits who oversee affairs of the heart, such as Ezili Dantor and Legba. However, despite her gracious and tender personality, Ezili Freda is also known for her caprice and temperamental behavior, which can cause conflict with other Loa. She is known to be particularly at odds with her darker counterpart, Ezili Dantor, who represents the other side of love, including jealousy and revenge. Additionally, her demanding nature and high expectations can create tension with other Loa, particularly those who do not meet her standards.

Despite these conflicts, Ezili Freda remains one of the most beloved and revered Loa in the Voodoo pantheon due to her ability to bring happiness, abundance, and harmony to the lives of those who honor her. The lore surrounding Ezili Freda is rich and varied. She is often described as a passionate and loving Loa who will go to great lengths to help those who call upon her. She is also known for her vanity and materialism, which can make her a challenging Loa to work with. It is said that she requires the finest offerings and gifts and that she can be quite particular in her tastes.

To honor Ezili Freda, practitioners of Voodoo often hold lavish parties and celebrations in her honor. These celebrations are filled with music, dancing, and offerings of champagne and sweet treats. In New Orleans, she is often celebrated during Mardi Gras and the annual Voodoo Festival.

Ezili Dantor

Ezili Dantor, Haiti's warrior and protector goddess, is one of the most powerful Loas in the Voodoo pantheon. She is known as a fierce defender of women and children, and her legend is steeped in bravery and tragedy. Ezili Dantor is often depicted as a black woman with scars and wearing a blue and red scarf around her head. She is armed with a machete and can be seen with a child at her feet or on her hip, which represents her maternal and protective nature. Her veve, the symbol used to invoke her energy, is typically drawn with a heart and a sword.

Ezili Dantor.
https://www.pxfuel.com/en/free-photo-oesnm

She is syncretized with the Catholic Saints, most often with the Black Madonna of Częstochowa, and is associated with the colors gold, green, red, and blue. Her offerings include rum, spicy food, and her favorite flower, the hibiscus. This Loa is known for her fiery and passionate nature, which makes her both a force to be reckoned with and a powerful protector. She is fiercely independent, and her independence is one of the main reasons she is so beloved by women. She is often associated with revolutionaries and is seen as an embodiment of the spirit of resistance.

Ezili Dantor has a complex relationship with her sister Loa, Ezili Freda. Although they are sisters, they have very different personalities and often clash with each other. Despite this, they are both associated with love and often invoked together to create a harmonious relationship. A powerful Loa, it is important that offerings to her are taken seriously. She is said to prefer offerings made in secret or in a private space, and those who make offerings to her must be pure of heart and intention. When she is pleased with an offering, it is said that she will protect and guide the person who made it.

Ezili Dantor is honored and celebrated in various ways throughout the year in New Orleans. One of the most popular celebrations is held on the day of Our Lady of Mount Carmel, July 26th. During this celebration, offerings are made to her, and her followers dance and sing in her honor. This Petro Loa is also honored during the Festival of the Dead and other Voodoo ceremonies.

Simbi

Simbi is a powerful Loa in Louisiana Voodoo, often associated with serpents and water. She is known to take on many forms but is most commonly depicted as a serpent with a woman's head or a woman with a serpent's tail. Her veve, a sacred symbol used in Voodoo rituals, features the image of a serpent with a wave-like pattern.

Simbi.

In Haitian Vodou, Simbi is often syncretized with Saint Patrick, who is said to have driven the snakes out of Ireland. Simbi is also associated with the Catholic Saint John the Baptist and is sometimes called "Simbi St. Jean."

The colors most commonly associated with Simbi are green and blue, and her corresponding plants include water lilies, cattails, and snakeroot. She is said to have dominion over rivers, streams, and other bodies of water and is often called upon for help with fertility, healing, and divination matters.

Simbi is known to have interesting connections to several other Loa, as her role and abilities overlap with theirs. For example, she is sometimes associated with the Loa Agwe, who is also a water spirit. In some traditions, she is seen as Agwe's wife; in others, they are considered two aspects of the same Loa. Similarly, Simbi is sometimes associated with the Loa Damballah, a serpent spirit. In some traditions, she is seen as Damballah's wife; in others, they are considered two aspects of the same Loa.

Simbi is also often associated with Loa Ayida Wedo, who is Damballah's female counterpart. Ayida Wedo is also a water spirit and is often depicted as a rainbow. Simbi and Ayida Wedo are sometimes seen as opposing forces, with Simbi representing water's dark, dangerous aspects and Ayida Wedo representing water's peaceful, life-giving aspects. In other traditions, however, they are seen as complementary forces, with Simbi representing the power and strength of water and Ayida Wedo representing its beauty and grace.

She is also sometimes associated with Loa Ezili, a spirit of love and sexuality. In some traditions, Simbi is seen as Ezili's husband; in others, they are considered two aspects of the same Loa. This association may reflect the fact that in Voudou, water is often associated with emotions and relationships.

Simbi's lore is rich and varied, with stories depicting her as compassionate and vengeful. She is said to be a wise teacher and healer but can also be dangerous when crossed. In one legend, she transformed a man into a snake after he insulted her. In another, she is used her power to create a healing spring for a sick child.

Offerings to Simbi vary depending on the situation but can include offerings of water, herbs, and candles. She appears to enjoy offerings of tobacco and rum and is often depicted with a cigar in her mouth. Signs that Simbi has received and accepted an offering can include the flickering of candles or water movement. In New Orleans, Simbi is often celebrated as part of the annual St. John's Eve celebration on June 23rd. This festival is a time to honor the relationship between Simbi and St. John the Baptist and is marked by bonfires, dancing, and other rituals. Simbi is also sometimes invoked during Mardi Gras and other Voodoo ceremonies throughout the year.

Gran Ibo

Gran Ibo, or Gran Yobo or Grannibo, is a powerful and enigmatic Loa in the Voodoo pantheon. Considered the "Mother of Nature," she is associated with the forces of the Earth, particularly with the trees and the mountains. Her image is of an elderly woman with a powerful presence, often depicted wearing a headdress made of leaves or branches and carrying a staff made of wood or metal.

Gran Ibo is considered to be mother nature.
https://unsplash.com/photos/hMYAVaOWSHc

The veve, or sacred symbol, of Gran Ibo, is a unique and intricate design that is often drawn on the ground with cornmeal or flour as a ritual invocation of her presence. The symbol features a central tree surrounded by several other elements, including a snake, a turtle, and a representation of the sun. Gran Ibo is syncretized with Saint Jerome, and her feast day is celebrated on September 30th. Her correspondences include green and brown colors, and her associated plants are oak, pine, and avocado.

As a Loa of nature and the wilderness, Gran Ibo is said to have close relationships with other earthy Loa, including Damballah, Simbi, and Agwe. She is also known for her ability to heal the sick and injured, particularly through the use of herbal remedies and spiritual cleansing. In Voodoo lore, Gran Ibo is often depicted as a powerful and wise figure who provides guidance and protection to those who seek her aid. She is known to be a strict but fair teacher, and those needing spiritual guidance often seek her wisdom.

To honor Gran Ibo, you can offer her candles, fruits, and flowers, particularly those associated with her, such as oak leaves and pine needles. Signs that she has accepted your offering may include the appearance of a snake or turtle or a sense of calm and balance in your surroundings. In New Orleans, Gran Ibo is celebrated as a vital force of nature, and her presence can be felt in the lush greenery of the city's many parks and gardens. She is often honored through public celebrations and rituals, particularly on her feast day. If you seek her wisdom and guidance, look to the natural world and allow her spirit to guide you on your journey.

Chapter Six: Major Male Loa

In this chapter, you will learn about the major male Loa in Louisiana Voodoo. Once more, please note that there's no way to cover every one of them in existence, so if there are some that you're interested in that aren't mentioned here, you should do some research. Having said that, it's time to check out the most accessible and popular male Loa.

Papa Legba

Papa Legba is the powerful gatekeeper and intermediary between the spirit and human worlds. In the realm of the Vodou, he is one of the most important and widely venerated Loa. He is often depicted as an elderly man but also as a young man with a limp. He is known for his smile, the kindness in his eyes, and the wisdom that emanates from his being. His image is often associated with the colors red and black. The veve, or ritual symbol, for Papa Legba, is a crossroads with a circle around it. He is considered the opener of the gates between the worlds.

This Loa is often syncretized with St. Peter in the Catholic religion, as both are gatekeepers. However, some also associate him with St. Lazarus or St. Anthony. He is closely associated with communication and language and is believed to be able to speak every human tongue. Some of the herbs associated with him include tobacco, coffee, and corn, while his corresponding colors include red and black.

As with most Loa, this one also has some fascinating ties to many of the others. He is often seen as the intermediary between the human and spiritual realms and is responsible for granting access to other spirits. In this role, he has developed intricate relationships with other Loa. For example, Papa Legba is often associated with the Loa Loco, who is the patron of healers and plants. Together, they are seen as the guardians of the crossroads and work together to maintain a balance between the worlds. Papa Legba also closely relates to Damballa, who represents the sky and creation. They work together to maintain balance in the natural world.

He also has a relationship with Ezili, particularly Loas Ezili Freda and Ezili Dantor. With Ezili Freda, they share an association with love and beauty and are often called upon together to bring blessings of fertility and prosperity. With Ezili Dantor, they share an association with motherhood and protection. They are often called upon together for help with familial issues. In addition, Papa Legba is connected to Baron Samedi, who is the lord of the dead. They are often seen as opposites, with Papa Legba representing life and light, while Baron Samedi represents death and darkness. Despite their differences, they are both seen as essential to maintaining the balance between life and death.

His role as the gatekeeper and intermediary between the worlds makes him integral to the Vodou tradition. He is often seen as the first and last Loa to be called upon during Vodou ceremonies, and all communication with the other Loa must pass through him.

Often depicted as playful and mischievous, he is also wise and powerful. He is said to protect children and have a great fondness for dancing and singing.

Offerings to Papa Legba can include rum, cigars, coffee, and candy. Some also offer keys, as he is known as the "key holder." Signs that he has received and accepted one's offering can include feeling his presence, such as hearing his voice or experiencing a sudden breeze. In New Orleans, Papa Legba is celebrated on the feast day of St. Anthony, which falls on June 13th. He is often honored with ritual offerings, dances, and ceremonies, as he is considered an important part of the local Vodou tradition.

Baron Samedi

Baron Samedi, the Loa of death, is a complex and fascinating figure in the Vodou tradition. He is often depicted as a skeleton in a black top hat, black coat, and dark glasses, with a cigar in his mouth and a bottle of rum in his hand. Despite his association with death, he is a beloved figure and brings joy and laughter to those who honor him.

His veve, a sacred symbol used in Vodou rituals, often features an image of a skull, crossed bones, and a top hat. His symbols also include a shovel, a black rooster, and a rattle made from human bones. In syncretic Catholicism, Baron Samedi is often identified with Saint Martin de Porres or Saint Expedite, but his true essence lies in the depths of the Vodou tradition. The color associated with Baron Samedi is black, representing death and the afterlife's mysteries. Plants and herbs associated with him include belladonna, tobacco, and wormwood, often used in rituals and offerings.

Baron Samedi is a member of the Ghede family of Loa, which is associated with death and fertility. He is often portrayed as the husband of Maman Brigitte, the Loa of death and cemeteries. He is also known for his close relationship with the Loa of healing and fertility, Ayizan, and the Loa of the crossroads, Papa Legba. Baron Samedi is known for his playful and mischievous personality. He is often depicted as a trickster, and his humor and wit are renowned among those who honor him. He is also known for his sexual prowess and is often seen as a symbol of fertility and virility.

Offerings to Baron Samedi typically include rum, cigars, and spicy foods. His offerings are often left at the entrance to cemeteries, which are his sacred spaces. Signs that he has accepted an offering may include the sound of laughter, the movement of objects, or the presence of the scent of rum or cigars. Baron Samedi is celebrated in New Orleans during the annual Vodou Festival and other Vodou ceremonies. He is also honored during the Day of the Dead, a celebration of the ancestors, which takes place in early November. The Baron is a powerful and enigmatic figure in the Vodou tradition. His association with death and the afterlife makes him both feared and revered, but his playful and humorous nature endears him to those who honor him.

Damballah

Damballah, the snake Loa of Haitian Vodou, is a powerful and revered deity who is often associated with creation, fertility, and the natural world. He is usually represented as a long, coiling serpent, often with a white or silver color and with a penchant for shedding its skin. Damballah is known to be a very old and wise Loa, often depicted as a great serpent in the sky, and is said to possess deep knowledge and wisdom about the mysteries of life and the universe.

The veve of Damballah is often portrayed as a serpent coiled around a pole, with symbols such as sunbursts, moon crescents, and stars surrounding it. His associated colors are white, silver, and pale blue, and he is linked to plants such as basil, thyme, and sage. Damballah's closest relation is his wife, Ayida Wedo, and the two are often depicted together in their cosmic dance, representing the cycle of creation and rebirth. Other Loa with which he is associated include Ogoun, the warrior Loa, and Legba, the gatekeeper. In Haitian Vodou lore, Damballah is known for his calm and serene demeanor, and his voice is said to be like a gentle breeze, carrying with it the secrets of the universe. He is also known for his great power, strength, and healing abilities and is sometimes called upon in times of illness or distress.

Offerings to Damballah usually consist of pure, clean water and white rum or other white liquors. He is also associated with eggs, as they symbolize fertility and new beginnings. Signs that he has received and accepted offerings include a feeling of peace and calmness and a sense of being in the presence of great wisdom and power. Voodooists celebrate Damballah during the annual Vodou festival, as well as during Mardi Gras and other cultural events. His followers will often dance and chant in his honor, offering prayers and gifts to this powerful and ancient Loa.

Agwe

Agwe, the Loa of the sea, is a powerful and enigmatic figure in the pantheon of Louisiana Voodoo. Known for his fierce loyalty and potent magic, he is revered by sailors, fishermen, and all who make their livelihoods on the waters. Agwe is said to appear as a dark-skinned man with a commanding presence, often dressed in naval or maritime attire. He is associated with the color blue; his symbols include anchors, shells, and fish. His veve is a complex and intricate design featuring waves, seahorses, and a depiction of his sacred vessel, the ship.

In some traditions, Agwe is syncretized with the Catholic saint St. Ulrich of Augsburg, who is said to have miraculous powers over water. However, many practitioners of Louisiana Voodoo view Agwe as a deity in his own right, not to be confused with any other figure. Agwe's correspondences include sea-related items, such as seaweed, coral, sea salt, and the colors blue and white. He is also associated with the herbs vetiver and angelica.

Agwe is connected to his wife, the goddess of love and beauty, Ezili Freda, Baron Samedi, and the Loa of death and rebirth. Agwe's status as a master of the sea often puts him at odds with the Loa of the earth and land, such as Papa Legba and Damballah. Bits of lore connected to Agwe paint him as a powerful and fiercely protective figure, willing to go to great lengths to defend his devotees. He is particularly fond of children, and offerings of toys and candy are often left at his altars as a sign of devotion.

Preferred offerings for Agwe include fish, seafood, and rum, often placed in his sacred vessel, which is kept on his altar. Signs that he has received and accepted an offering may include movement or activity from the sacred vessel and dreams or visions of the sea. Agwe's devotees celebrate him in various ways, including a yearly boat procession down the Mississippi River, known as the Blessing of the Fleet. This event often includes offerings to Agwe and other Loa and traditional music, dancing, and feasting. Devotees may also honor Agwe at home altars or in community gatherings, particularly those associated with the sea or water.

Loko

Loko, the Loa of vegetation, is a powerful spirit who plays an important role in Louisiana Voodoo. He is often depicted as a tall, thin man, wearing a suit made of green leaves and holding a hoe or a machete. Loko's appearance reflects his connection to nature and his role as a farmer who cultivates the land and provides food for the people. Loko's veve, or sacred symbol, is a series of interconnected lines and circles, often depicted in green and brown. This veve is used in ceremonies to invoke Loko's presence and blessings.

In Louisiana Voodoo, Loko is often syncretized with Saint Isidore, the patron saint of farmers. This association highlights the agricultural aspect of Loko's character and his importance in providing for the people. Loko's correspondences include the colors green and brown, as well as plants like corn, beans, and squash, which are traditionally grown together in Native American agriculture. These plants represent Loko's role as a cultivator and provider of sustenance. He has a close relationship with other Loa of agriculture and fertility, such as Ayizan, the Loa of the marketplace, and Azaka, the Loa of the harvest. Together, they ensure the land is fertile, and the people are fed.

You need to beware of this Loa's quick temper and tendency to act impulsively. In some stories, he is portrayed as stubborn and difficult to work with but also fiercely protective of those who honor him. His personality reflects the unpredictability of nature and the challenges faced by those who depend on the land for survival.

To honor Loko, fresh produce offerings, especially corn, are often left at the crossroads or in other outdoor spaces. Signs that Loko has received and accepted an offering may include the rustling of leaves, the sudden appearance of a breeze, or the sound of a hoe striking the ground. Loko is often celebrated in New Orleans during the annual Voodoo Festival and in smaller, more private ceremonies throughout the year. During these ceremonies, participants may sing and dance in honor of Loko, invoking his power to bring abundance and fertility to the land.

Azaka

Azaka, also known as Azaka Medeh, is a Loa associated with agriculture and the earth. He is believed to be a powerful spirit who can bless crops, bring rain, and help the people who rely on the land for their livelihood. He is a tall, muscular man with a muscular physique and the strength of an ox. He is often depicted wearing a straw hat and holding a machete, both symbols of his connection to agriculture. Azaka's veve is a complex symbol that includes the image of a plow and other agricultural tools. It is usually drawn in white on a background of green, which symbolizes fertility and growth.

This powerful Loa is syncretized with Saint Isidore, the patron saint of farmers. This syncretism reflects the importance of agriculture in Haitian society and how traditional beliefs have been incorporated into the practice of Catholicism in Haiti. The colors associated with Azaka are green, brown, and yellow, and his favorite offerings include corn, beans, and other agricultural products. His herbs include basil, vervain, and mugwort, believed to have spiritual and medicinal properties.

Azaka is closely associated with his brother, Guede, who is the Loa of death and the underworld. Together, the two brothers form a powerful duo who are believed to have the ability to bring fertility and abundance to the land. In Haitian Vodou, Azaka is believed to have a jovial and generous personality. He is often seen as a kind and benevolent spirit willing to help those in need. He is especially revered by farmers and those who rely on the land for their livelihood.

To honor Azaka, people often create altars and offer him gifts of food, drink, and tobacco. They may also perform rituals and dances in his honor, particularly during the planting and harvest seasons. In New Orleans, Azaka is celebrated during the annual Vodou Festival, which takes place in the city's historic French Quarter. During the festival, participants pay tribute to the Loa through music, dance, and other forms of artistic expression.

Ogou

Ogou, the powerful warrior Loa of Vodou, is known for his strength, courage, and unyielding character. A fierce protector and defender of the people, he is often invoked for his abilities in battle and as a mediator in disputes. In Vodou tradition, Ogou is often depicted as a handsome, strong, and virile man, dressed in military regalia, with weapons in his hands and a fierce countenance. His image is often associated with red, symbolizing his passion, power, and energy.

The veve of Ogou is a complex symbol, representing his warrior status and association with fire, lightning, and thunder. It is often drawn in a trident shape, symbolizing the three aspects of Ogou; the fiery warrior, the cool-headed mediator, and the deep, wise spirit. Ogou is associated with St. James the Greater in some syncretic traditions, and his feast day is celebrated on July 25th. As a warrior saint, St. James shares many characteristics with Ogou, and many of the stories associated with St. James have been adapted into the mythology of Ogou.

In terms of correspondence, Ogou is often associated with the color red and iron, steel, and other metals. His favorite offerings include rum, cigars, spicy foods, swords, knives, and other weapons. He is also associated with the herb basil, which is said to have protective properties and is often used in offerings and rituals to honor Ogou. Ogou is known to have complex relationships with other Loa. He is often associated with Shango's fiery and passionate spirit and is sometimes seen as a rival to the more seductive and sensual Lwa, Legba. He is also closely connected to the Earth and its elemental forces. He is sometimes associated with the Loa of the crossroads, Papa Legba.

In terms of lore, Ogou is known for his bravery, strength, and keen sense of justice and fairness. He is often called upon to protect the vulnerable and defend the weak and is sometimes associated with the image of the knight in shining armor. When devotees want to honor this Loa, there are many different rituals and practices associated with this powerful and revered Loa. Offerings of rum, tobacco, and spicy foods are often made to Ogou, and he is sometimes invoked in ceremonies involving swords and other weapons. Ogou is often celebrated in New Orleans during Mardi Gras, when many Vodou practitioners honor his powerful and protective spirit with parades, music, and dance.

Ti-Jean Petro

Ti-Jean Petro is a Loa in Louisiana Voodoo who embodies youth, vitality, and the fiery spirit of rebellion. He is often invoked by those seeking to overcome obstacles, stand up for themselves, and make a change in their lives. In appearance, he is often depicted as a young man with dark skin and a muscular build. He may carry a sword, machete, or another weapon and is often seen with a red bandanna or scarf tied around his head. His veve is a complex, interlocking geometric pattern representing his fiery nature and determination. The veve is typically drawn in red or black and is often accompanied by symbols of other Loa with whom Ti-Jean Petro has close connections, such as Papa Legba, Ezili Dantor, and Baron Samedi.

As a Petro Loa, Ti-Jean Petro is not syncretized with any Catholic saints and is instead worshipped in his own right. This Loa's correspondences include red and black and herbs and plants like red pepper, ginger, and tobacco. He is also associated with the elements of fire and water, which symbolize his dual nature as both a fiery spirit of rebellion and a protector of the community. Regarding his relationships with other Loa, Ti-Jean Petro is often seen as a companion to the warrior Loa Ogou. He is also closely connected to Ezili Dantor, the fierce and protective mother figure often invoked by women seeking help with matters of love and protection. Lore connected to Ti-Jean Petro depicts him as a fiery and rebellious spirit who is not afraid to stand up for himself or others. He is known for his fierce determination and willingness to fight for justice and equality.

Offerings of red and black candles, rum, and cigars are often made to honor Ti-Jean Petro. Some practitioners also offer spicy foods, such as hot sauce, to recognize his association with the element of fire. Signs that he has received and accepted your offering may include candles that burn brightly and steadily and a sense of inner strength and determination. Ti-Jean Petro is often celebrated during the annual Voodoo Festival in New Orleans, where he is invoked in ritual and honored with offerings of rum and cigars. In addition, he is often invoked during personal ceremonies and rites, where he is called upon to help individuals overcome obstacles and achieve their goals.

Chapter Seven: Creating Your Voodoo Altar

The Importance of Your Voodoo Altar

You don't have to have a shrine or an altar in your house, but the thing is that having one will increase and strengthen your connection to the spirits. You'll be able to feel them more in your life, and this is a good thing. In the practice of Voodoo, altars are considered the heart and soul of one's spiritual space. They are the place where you can connect the divine, a physical representation of your innermost beliefs, and a visual reminder of the importance of your spiritual practice.

A voodoo altar.
https://www.flickr.com/photos/mark-gunn/39651373500

Your altar is your sacred space, and it can be as simple or as elaborate as you want it to be. It can be a small shelf or a large table, and it can hold various items significant to you and your spiritual practice. Altars are a place of worship and reflection where you can seek guidance, solace, or simply a moment of peace.

In Voodoo, altars are not just places to display beautiful objects or decorative pieces. They are a focal point of your practice, where you can offer prayers, make offerings, and invite the spirits to come and dwell with you. You can adorn your altar with candles, flowers, crystals, and other sacred objects that have meaning for you.

It is also important to remember that an altar is a living thing. It is a reflection of your relationship with the spirits, and it must be tended to with care and reverence. You can clean your altar, refresh the offerings, and adjust the placement of items to create a harmonious and peaceful environment. Creating an altar is not just about displaying beautiful objects. A spiritual act of devotion deepens your connection to the divine. It is a space where you can feel free to be yourself, express your hopes and fears, and seek guidance and support. You can light a candle, offer some incense, and sit in quiet contemplation, knowing that you are never alone and the spirits are always with you. So, as you embark on your Voodoo journey, remember the importance of creating a sacred space where you can connect with the spirits. Your altar is a place of reverence, a visual representation of your spiritual practice, and a reminder of the divine presence that surrounds you always.

Choosing a Sacred Space

Creating a Voodoo altar is a sacred act that requires intention and mindfulness. The first step in this process is choosing the perfect space for your altar. You should look for a place that feels peaceful, where you can spend time reflecting and connecting with the spirit world. When selecting a location for your altar, you should consider the energy of the space. Does it feel calm and soothing, or is it chaotic and cluttered? You want to create an altar in a sacred and harmonious space.

Another important consideration is privacy. You want to choose a space where you can set up your altar and perform your rituals without being disturbed. This space should be dedicated solely to your spiritual practice, so you can focus your energy and intentions without any distractions. Remember, the space you choose will be the home of your

Voodoo altar, a place where you will connect with the divine and communicate with the spirits. Choosing a location that feels safe, secure, and welcoming is important. So, take your time, and choose the space that speaks to you. It could be a quiet corner of your bedroom, a cozy nook in your living room, or a peaceful spot in your garden. Wherever you choose, make sure it feels right to you and that it's a space you can dedicate to your spiritual practice for years to come.

Materials Needed

You may wonder why you must create an altar for your Voodoo practice. The answer is simple: it depends on your personal preferences and the Loa with whom you wish to work. However, you can follow some general guidelines to ensure you have what you need.

First of all, it's important to know where to get the materials for your altar. Many items can be found at your local spiritual or metaphysical shop or even online. You can also find items in nature, such as branches, stones, and herbs. But no matter where you get your items, it's important to make sure they are of good quality and resonate with you and your practice. Please note that the items that are required for a Voodoo altar vary, and the items used can depend on the specific tradition or the Loa being honored. However, some common items are typically found on a Voodoo altar.

The centerpiece of a Voodoo altar is usually a large candle, which represents the light of the Loa. The candle should be placed in the center of the altar and should be the tallest item on the altar. The color of the candle can vary depending on the Loa being honored.

The altar itself can be covered with a colored cloth, either red or white, to honor the Petro Loa, or the Rada Loa, respectively.

You can have decorative items like statues, flowers, roots, amulets, talismans, stones, and anything else you resonate with. You'll also want some incense, oils, and even perfumes. Other items that are commonly found on a Voodoo altar include:

- **Water:** Representing the element of water, which is associated with the Loa, water is usually placed in a small dish or bowl on the altar. This water has to be changed every day.

- **Offerings:** Offerings can include food, drink, tobacco, or other items that are pleasing to the Loa. The specific offerings can vary depending on the Loa being honored.

- **Veve:** You should have the religious symbols representing the Loa you are working with.

- **Gris-gris bags:** Gris-gris bags are small bags filled with herbs, roots, stones, and other objects that are believed to have magical properties. They are often used for protection, luck, or to attract love. You can place the ones that serve your needs on the altar.

- **Ancestral altar:** An ancestral altar is a separate altar dedicated to honoring the spirits of the practitioner's ancestors. It is typically placed near the main Voodoo altar and may include items such as photographs of ancestors, candles, and offerings.

A general rule of thumb is that if something is connected to any of the Loa you're working with or has a deep significance to you and brings you in touch with your spiritual side, you can put it on the altar to enhance its power. Note that you can use a shelf, table, or even a cabinet to set up your altar. You can put up pictures of the Loa, their veves, or the saints with which they are syncretized to draw their energy to your altar. Set a white candle on one side of the altar and a red one on the other side. A bell is another useful item because it immediately raises the vibration of the place when you ring it, and it helps to get rid of any unwanted spirits lurking around.

Blessing and Cleansing Your Items

It is important to cleanse and bless the items you will use to set up your altar. Cleansing removes any negative energy or impurities that may be present while blessing infuses the items with positive energy and the power of the spirits. One cleansing method is to use smoke from burning herbs, such as sage or palo santo. To do this, light the herbs and allow the smoke to permeate the items, saying a prayer or incantation as you do so. For example, you could say, "Great spirits of the earth and sky, cleanse these items and make them pure. Let them be a sacred offering to you."

Another method of cleansing is to use salt water. Fill a bowl with water and add a handful of sea salt. Then, dip each item into the salt water and say a prayer or incantation, such as "May the power of the ocean wash away any negativity from these items and bless them with the power of the sea." A third method of cleansing is to bury the items in the earth. Find a spot outside, dig a small hole, and bury the items for a few days. This allows the earth to absorb any negative energy and infuse the items with positive energy. When you dig up the items, say a prayer or incantation such as "Great Mother Earth, bless these items with the power of the Earth and the spirits of the land."

Once the items have been cleansed, it is important to bless them. One way to do this is to use holy water or a blessing oil. Simply dip your fingers into the water or oil and make the sign of the cross or other symbol on each item. As you do this, say a prayer or incantation, such as "May these items be blessed by the spirits and be filled with the power of the divine."

Alternatively, you could use a crystal or other charged object. Hold the crystal in your hand and place the items on top of it, reciting a prayer or incantation, such as "May the power of this crystal bless these items and infuse them with positive energy and the power of the spirits." Suppose you would like a different way to bless the items. In that case, you could use a ritual or ceremony, such as a full moon ceremony or a prayer circle. Gather together with like-minded individuals and say prayers or incantations, asking the spirits to bless the items and fill them with positive energy.

You may be wondering, "What's the big deal if I don't cleanse and bless these things? Why can't I just set up my altar and be done with it?" In Louisiana Voodoo, it is believed that everything has spiritual energy or essence, including the items on your altar. Suppose these items are not properly cleansed and blessed. In that case, they can carry negative or stagnant energy, which can interfere with the effectiveness of your altar and the power of your rituals. Without proper cleansing, any negative energy or intentions which may have been associated with the item, whether during manufacturing or prior usage, could affect your altar negatively. Also, if you do not bless your altar items, you may be missing out on their full potential, as it is believed the items themselves have a spiritual essence and can contribute to the effectiveness of your altar and rituals.

Additionally, not properly caring for your altar items can be seen as a lack of respect for the spirits and the practice of Voodoo. This lack of respect and attention to detail can sometimes be seen as disrespectful and may even offend the spirits or ancestors being honored on the altar. So, you have to give proper attention and care to the items on your altar, as they play an integral role in your practice and relationship with the spirits. Properly cleansing and blessing your altar items ensures that they are ready to be used for your rituals and contribute to your practice's overall effectiveness.

Frequently Asked Questions

What is an altar?

An altar is a sacred space to connect with the spirits, ancestors, and the Loa.

Do I need an altar to practice Voodoo?

No, you do not need an altar to practice Voodoo, but it is highly recommended as it provides a focal point for your spiritual practice.

Can I have multiple altars?

Yes, you can have multiple altars for different purposes or to honor different spirits or Loa.

How do I choose a location for my altar?

Choose a location that is quiet and private, where you can focus on your spiritual practice without distraction.

What items should I have on my altar?

The items you should have on your altar depend on the Loa or spirits you are working with, but some common items include candles, water, flowers, statues or pictures of the Loa or spirits, and offerings such as food or drink.

Can I dedicate one altar to two Loa?

Yes, you can dedicate one altar to multiple Loa if they have a strong connection or if they work well together.

Should anyone besides me use my altar?

No, your altar is a personal and sacred space and should only be used by you and those you trust.

Can I decorate my altar with non-traditional items?

Yes, you can decorate your altar with items that have personal significance to you as long as they do not contradict Voodoo's spiritual beliefs and practices.

How do I maintain my altar?

You should regularly clean and tidy your altar, change the water and offerings, and replace any items that have become worn or damaged.

Can I move my altar to a different location?

Yes, you can move your altar to a different location if needed, but you should cleanse and bless the items and space again after the move.

Can I have an outdoor altar?

Yes, you can have an outdoor altar, but you should protect it from the elements and be mindful of any local laws or regulations.

Can I have an altar in a shared space?

Yes, you can have an altar in a shared space, but you should respect the beliefs and practices of those around you and keep the altar clean and tidy.

Can I use a temporary altar?

Yes, you can use a temporary altar if you need to, such as when traveling or if you do not have a permanent space.

Can I have a virtual altar?

Yes, you can have a virtual altar, such as a digital image or a website, but it should still be treated with respect and maintained as you would a physical altar.

How often should I cleanse and bless my altar items?

You should cleanse and bless your altar items regularly, such as once a week or before and after important rituals or offerings.

What is the purpose of cleansing and blessing my altar items?

Cleansing and blessing your altar items remove negative or unwanted energies and imbue them with positive, protective energies to enhance your spiritual practice.

How do I cleanse my altar items?

You can cleanse your altar items using methods such as smoke cleansing with sage or palo santo, saltwater baths, or placing them in direct sunlight or moonlight.

How do I bless my altar items?

You can bless your altar items by speaking prayers or incantations over them, anointing them with oils or holy water, or exposing them to sacred energies or symbols.

Can I use store-bought items on my altar?

Yes, you can use store-bought items. Just make sure you cleanse them first and bless them as well.

Can I keep my altar in a closet or other enclosed space?

It's generally recommended to keep your altar in a space that is open and easily accessible to allow the spirits to interact with it. However, if you need to keep it in a closet or other enclosed space for practical reasons, you can still work with it. Just be careful when working with lit candles.

Can I use herbs and other natural materials for my altar?

Yes, using herbs and other natural materials is a common practice in Voodoo. Just make sure to properly cleanse and bless them before using them on your altar.

Can I use animal bones or other animal parts on my altar?

Using animal bones or other animal parts is a common practice in some forms of Voodoo, but it's important to make sure that the animals are ethically sourced and that you have the proper knowledge and respect for working with them.

Can I use objects from other spiritual practices on my altar?

While some objects from other spiritual practices may be appropriate for your altar, it's important to make sure that they are compatible with Voodoo and that you cleanse and bless them appropriately.

Can I create an altar for a specific purpose or intention, such as healing or prosperity?

Yes, creating an altar for a specific purpose or intention is a common practice in Voodoo. Just make sure to choose items that are appropriate for your intention and to properly cleanse and bless them.

Can I use my altar for divination or other spiritual practices?

Yes, your altar can be used for divination, prayer, and other spiritual practices. Just make sure to properly cleanse and bless the items before using them for each purpose.

Can I use one altar for the Rada and Petro Loa pantheons at the same time?

Please don't do this, as both pantheons are completely different and do not work together like this. You should have different altars, or at the very least, there should be a very clear demarcation on your altar to show one side is for the Petro and the other for the Rada.

Chapter Eight: You and the Wisdom of Your Ancestors

The importance of ancestors in Louisiana Voodoo cannot be overstated. In fact, the practice is founded upon the veneration and worship of those who came before. Ancestors are seen as a bridge between the spiritual and physical realms, a sacred and powerful connection.

In Louisiana Voodoo, the spirits of the ancestors are honored and respected for their guidance, protection, and wisdom. They are believed to watch over their descendants and offer support, love, and blessings to those who honor them. It is believed that your ancestors can impact your life in profound ways, positively or negatively.

Connecting with the elders and the ancestors is crucial to voodoo practice.
https://www.flickr.com/photos/africa-rising/26226168738

Through ancestor worship, the Voodooist seeks to cultivate a relationship with those who have gone before them, tapping into their knowledge and experience to guide them in their own journeys. In turn, devotees offer the ancestors love, respect, and acknowledgment, honoring their presence in their lives and the impact they continue to have on them. The importance of ancestors is evident in the very fabric of Louisiana Voodoo. The use of ancestral altars, rituals, and offerings is a key aspect of the tradition. These altars are adorned with photographs, candles, flowers, and other items that connect you with your ancestors. You can communicate with your ancestors through these offerings, showing them your love and respect and seeking their guidance and wisdom.

The Role of Ancestors

Ancestors play an essential role in the practice, with different types of ancestors being acknowledged and revered. These ancestors include blood, spiritual, and cultural ancestors, and each holds a unique role in the individual's spiritual and physical existence.

Blood ancestors: Blood ancestors are those who are biologically related to the individual, such as grandparents, parents, and siblings. In Louisiana Voodoo, the blood ancestors are believed to watch over and guide their descendants. The individual can access their wisdom and guidance by acknowledging and venerating them.

Spiritual ancestors: These ancestors are those who are not biologically related to the individual but are instead connected through spiritual lineage. They may include Voodoo practitioners, community leaders, or influential spiritual figures. In Louisiana Voodoo, spiritual ancestors are believed to offer their spiritual descendants protection, guidance, and blessings.

Cultural ancestors: Cultural ancestors are those who are connected to the individual through their cultural heritage, such as being African, Native American, or European ancestors. They offer a connection to the individual's roots, heritage, and history and can provide insights into the cultural practices that have shaped their spiritual and physical identity.

Each type of ancestor plays a significant role in the individual's life and spiritual practice, offering a unique perspective and guidance. By acknowledging and venerating each type of ancestor, the individual can develop a deeper connection to their spiritual and cultural heritage and access the wisdom and blessings of those who came before them.

How Your Ancestors Help You

They offer you guidance: Your ancestors can offer guidance in making decisions and navigating life's challenges. They have a wealth of knowledge and experience that they can offer you. They have lived through similar situations and challenges you may be facing and have gained wisdom and insight they can share with you.

By connecting with your ancestors, you are tapping into a source of guidance that can help you make decisions and navigate life's challenges. Your ancestors can guide you in many ways, such as through dreams, intuition, and signs in the physical world. They may also communicate with you through divination tools like tarot cards, pendulums, or spirit boards. These methods can offer you insights, advice, and support to help you make the best decisions for yourself and your life.

They protect you: Your ancestors can offer protection against negative energies and harm. Your ancestors have the power to protect you from negative energies and harm. This protection comes in many forms, including physical, emotional, and spiritual protection. Ancestors can help shield you from danger and negative influences and offer comfort and support when you feel vulnerable or alone.

When you connect with your ancestors, you open up a channel for their protective energy to flow into your life. Inviting them into your practice and dedicating space on your altar for them creates a sacred bond, allowing them to watch over you and keep you safe. Ancestors can also offer protection by helping you recognize and avoid dangerous situations. They benefit from experience and wisdom from their own lives.

They'll help you grow spiritually: Connecting with your ancestors can help you on your spiritual journey and aid in your personal growth. In Louisiana Voodoo, spiritual growth is highly valued and essential to the practice. Ancestors are believed to be highly spiritual beings who have passed on to the spirit world and can guide their descendants on their own spiritual journey. By connecting with their ancestors, Voodoo practitioners can gain valuable insights, wisdom, and understanding of spiritual practices and teachings passed down through generations.

Ancestors, especially those known to be highly spiritual or religious leaders, are believed to have acquired a great deal of spiritual knowledge and experience that can be passed down to their descendants. Through ancestral communication, a practitioner can receive guidance, advice, and teachings that help them develop spiritually and gain a deeper understanding of their spiritual path. Ancestors can also provide reassurance and comfort, helping practitioners find their way during difficult times. Through ancestral communication, you can gain insight into your strengths and weaknesses and identify areas where you need to focus your efforts to continue to grow spiritually. This can lead to deeper self-awareness and help you move forward on your spiritual journey with greater confidence and clarity.

They can help you with manifestation: Your ancestors can assist in manifesting your goals and desires. The ancestors are powerful spiritual beings, able to intervene in the lives of their living descendants. They have a deep connection to the spiritual realm and can act as intermediaries between the physical and spiritual worlds. As a result, they can assist in manifesting the goals and desires of their living descendants. When you connect with your ancestors, you are tapping into the power of your lineage and calling upon your forebears' spiritual strength and abilities. Your ancestors can provide guidance and support to achieve your goals and desires. By working in partnership with them, you can call upon your ancestors to help manifest your intentions.

For example, suppose you're seeking financial abundance. In that case, it's a good idea to connect with those of your ancestors who were known for their business acumen or wealth. You can make offerings and request that your ancestors to guide and bless your financial endeavors. In this way, the ancestors can help to manifest your desires for abundance and success. Your ancestors can be co-creators of your reality along with you if you let them. Working with them is an easier way to live life than going it on your own. You should seek them out not only when you need something; instead, call on them all the time so that the connection between you stays strong.

Rituals for Connecting with Ancestors

Now it's time to connect with your ancestors. Keep in mind that you can switch up your Voodoo altar to make it fit for connecting with your ancestors simply by placing items on it that are reminiscent of them and their interests or that carry their energy. For instance, if you have an item from a late parent or grandparent, you can place it on the altar. The same goes for their photographs. You can also use them as a point of contact for every other ancestor who has passed on before them. With that said, the following are practical rituals that you can use to get in touch with them whenever you need to.

Ancestor Altar Ritual

1. Choose a space for your ancestor altar, such as a corner in your room or a special shelf.
2. Gather materials for your altar, including a white cloth, candles, incense, photos of your ancestors, and any offerings you wish to make.
3. Cleanse and bless your altar items before placing them on the altar, starting with the white cloth on the altar's surface and then placing everything else on it in an orderly fashion. Leave room in the middle of the altar for any item you may want to interact with, so you can set it there and move it aside when done.
4. Light the candles and incense and invite your ancestors to join you by saying a prayer or incantation. Your prayer doesn't have to be anything complex. You could just say, *"My ancestors, you who were here before I drew my first breath, I invite you here and now. Thank you for gracing me with your presence. Thank you for your rapt attention to my desires and for answers to my prayers."*
5. Now, give them any offerings you have chosen. You may do so by simply lifting each one in the air in their honor and placing it on the Center of the altar.
6. If you have anything you'd like to share with them or ask them, now's the time to do so. When you've finished, trust that they've heard you, and you'll get an answer. Also, be sure to thank them.

Ancestor Graveyard Ritual

1. Choose a grave of an ancestor or a local cemetery.
2. Bring offerings such as flowers, candles, food, and drink to leave at the grave.
3. Light candles and incense to create a sacred atmosphere.
4. Speak to your ancestor and offer your gifts and intentions.
5. Listen for any messages or guidance from your ancestor.

6. Thank your ancestor before leaving the cemetery.

Suppose you find cemeteries creepy, but you have an item that once belonged to an ancestor, or you have a picture of them. In that case, you can perform steps 2 to 6 with the image or item. That will also be good enough.

Ancestor Meditation Ritual

1. Find a quiet and comfortable place to sit in front of your ancestor's altar.

2. Light some incense or a candle to create a sacred atmosphere.

3. Close your eyes and take a few deep breaths to center yourself.

4. Visualize a bright light surrounding you, and then imagine your ancestors standing around you, encircling you in their energy.

5. Take a moment to feel their presence and connect with them.

6. Ask your ancestors to share any guidance, wisdom, or messages they have for you.

7. Listen for their response through intuition, visions, or even audible messages. Note that you may not get a response right away. Alternatively, you can just sit and bask in the feeling of appreciation and anticipation that the answer will come to you eventually, either during your meditation or at some point later.

8. When you feel ready, thank your ancestors for their presence and guidance, and offer them water, flowers, or food.

9. Slowly open your eyes and return to the present moment.

Please remember that when it comes to ancestor meditation, "your mileage may vary." Everyone has different experiences, and the odds are you'll need to practice this more than once to connect with your ancestors. So don't be hard on yourself if you feel nothing happened after one try. Consistency, patience, and trust are vital.

Tips for Remaining in Touch

1. Keep a picture of your ancestor on your altar or in a special place in your home where you can see it often. You could have it at the door, so you have to say hello before you leave the house each day.

2. Light a candle or burn some incense in honor of your ancestor every day or on special occasions.

3. Create a special offering for your ancestor, such as a favorite food or drink, and place it on your altar or at their grave site. You could do this weekly. If it's food or drink, you should leave it on the altar for some time, either overnight or just for some hours. Then you can get rid of it by throwing it outside to release the offering to your ancestors.

4. Set aside time each day to meditate and connect with your ancestors. Make this non-negotiable, kind of like brushing your teeth.

5. Write a letter to your ancestor and express your thoughts and feelings. You can either burn it or keep it as a keepsake in a special box dedicated to them. Assume that they will handle whatever you write about that goes into that box.

6. Ask your ancestor for guidance or advice when faced with difficult decisions.

7. Keep a journal to document any signs or messages from your ancestor.

8. Visit your ancestor's grave and bring flowers or other offerings.

9. Create an ancestral altar where you can honor your ancestors and keep their memory alive.

10. Share stories and traditions about your ancestors with your family and friends to keep their memory alive for future generations.

Ethics and Responsibilities of Working with Ancestors

In Louisiana Voodoo, working with ancestors is considered a sacred practice that carries ethical and moral responsibilities. It is believed that when you ask for the help of your ancestors, they respond in kind and offer guidance and protection. However, it is important to remember that with this privilege comes a responsibility to honor and respect your ancestors and their traditions.

One of the most important ethical considerations when working with ancestors is to be clear about your intentions and always ask for their consent before engaging in any rituals or practices. You should never force or coerce your ancestors into doing anything that goes against their will or beliefs. Another key responsibility is to maintain a high level of respect and reverence for your ancestors. This can be done through consistent offerings, such as lighting candles or incense on your altar and regularly performing rituals and prayers in their honor. It is also important to remember that your ancestors may have their own personalities and preferences, and it is important to honor and respect those differences. For example, some ancestors may prefer certain offerings or may not respond well to certain rituals or practices.

Finally, it is crucial to remember that working with ancestors is a two-way street. Just as you seek their guidance and protection, offering them your gratitude and appreciation is important. This can be done through regular offerings and acts of service, such as volunteering or making a charitable donation in their honor.

Now that you understand the importance of involving your ancestors in your daily life as a Voodooist, it's time to look at some of the important items in Voodoo that have been greatly misunderstood – so you know exactly how to make them work for you.

The next chapter will shed light on charms and more.

Chapter Nine: Voodoo Dolls and Charms

So, if you've learned anything about Voodoo, you probably already know about the Voodoo doll, the most popular of the charms. However, other charms are part of New Orleans Voodoo, and you're going to learn about them and more in this chapter.

Voodoo dolls.
https://www.flickr.com/photos/59489479@N08/17940796562

The Voodoo Doll

You must have heard of the Voodoo doll before, the tiny rag doll used to cast spells or cause harm to someone. But the reality of Voodoo dolls is quite different from the stereotype portrayed in movies and TV shows. A Voodoo doll is a handmade doll representing a person, typically used for healing, blessing, or protection. The doll is imbued with the energy of the person it represents and is believed to be a physical manifestation of that person. It is not used to cause harm or cast spells but to help connect with the person the doll represents.

Historically, in West Africa, dolls were used in religious ceremonies to represent ancestors or deities. When enslaved Africans were brought to the Americas, they brought their spiritual traditions with them, including the use of dolls in religious practices. Over time, the use of dolls evolved and adapted to the new environment and eventually became an integral part of Louisiana Voodoo. Unfortunately, the portrayal of Voodoo dolls in popular culture has created a number of misconceptions. Many people believe that Voodoo dolls are used to cause harm or control others, but this is simply not true. Louisiana Voodoo is a religion that emphasizes healing, protection, and connection with ancestors and spirits, not harm or manipulation. So, the next time you see a Voodoo doll in a movie or on TV, remember that it's not an accurate representation of the beautiful and complex spiritual practices of Louisiana Voodoo.

Gris-Gris

A gris-gris is a very powerful charm used in Louisiana Voodoo. It's a small bag filled with various objects, such as herbs, stones, and other curios, that are believed to hold spiritual power. This charm is used for various purposes, including protection, luck, love, and even to cause harm to an enemy. Gris-gris is rooted in African spiritual traditions that were brought to the Americas during the slave trade. The practice of using charms or amulets to protect oneself from evil spirits or bad luck has been around for centuries, and gris-gris is just one of many examples.

One common misconception about gris-gris is that it's always used for evil purposes. While it's true that gris-gris can be used to cause harm to an enemy, it's often used for more positive purposes, such as protection and luck. Another misconception is that gris-gris bags are always made by a Voodoo priest or priestess. While it's true that some gris-gris bags are made by practitioners with special training, it's also possible to make your own gris-gris at home.

So, don't be afraid of gris-gris. It's a fascinating and powerful charm that can be used for a variety of purposes. Just make sure that you're using it for the right reasons and with the proper guidance.

Mojo Bags

First, a mojo bag is not a cute little accessory to add to your outfit; it is a powerful tool used in Louisiana Voodoo and hoodoo traditions. A mojo bag is essentially a small, magical bag that contains certain ingredients, such as herbs, roots, crystals, or personal items, which are believed to bring luck, protection, love, or any other desired outcome. These bags are also known as "mojo hands" or "conjure bags," depending on the specific tradition.

In the past, slaves and other marginalized groups used mojo bags for protection and empowerment. They would create these bags using whatever materials they had on hand, including herbs, roots, and personal items such as hair or clothing. They believed carrying these bags would help them overcome obstacles and bring good luck. However, despite its historical significance, there are still some common misconceptions about mojo bags; just like gris-gris, some assume mojo bags are bad news. The truth is you can use them for either good or bad. It all comes down to your intentions, which are hopefully good.

Materials and Tools for Crafting Charms

When it comes to making charms, whether that's a Voodoo doll, gris-gris, or mojo bag, there are a variety of materials that you can use to create something very powerful and effective. Some common materials include:

- **Herbs:** Different herbs can represent different things, such as rosemary for protection or lavender for healing.

- **Oils:** Essential oils can anoint the charm and imbue it with certain energies or properties.

- **Stones:** Crystals and other stones can enhance the doll's energy and add specific qualities, such as amethyst for spiritual protection or citrine for abundance.

- **Cloth:** The color of the cloth you choose can also have significance. For example, red cloth may be used for love or passion, while green for prosperity.

- **Charms:** Small trinkets can be added to the Voodoo doll, gris-gris, or mojo bag to enhance its power. For example, a small key could be added to attract success or money. You can also add other charms together to give it more oomph.

- **Other materials:** Other materials that you may want to consider include feathers, shells, or other items that hold personal significance to you.

In addition to materials, you will also need some tools to create your Voodoo doll. Some common tools include:

- **Needle and thread:** You'll need these to sew the doll, mojo bag, or gris-gris together.

- **Scissors:** These will be necessary to cut the fabric and any other materials you'll be using.

- **Pins:** Pins can help hold things in place as you sew.

- **Stuffing:** You'll need something to stuff your doll with. Some people use cotton or other soft materials, while others prefer herbs or other materials to give the doll additional supernatural properties.

- **Mortar and pestle:** Used to grind herbs into a fine powder.

- **Anointing tool:** This could be a small brush. You could also just use a finger to anoint the charm with oil.

Choosing the appropriate materials is key to creating an effective charm. You'll want to consider your intentions and choose materials that align with your goals. For example, suppose you're making a charm for protection. In that case, you may want to choose materials like angelica root and chili peppers, which are known for their protective properties. If you're making a charm for love, you may want to choose materials like rose petals or rose oil – which are associated with love and romance. Remember, the more intentional you are with your materials, the more powerful your charm will be.

How to Make a Voodoo Doll

Materials:

- A piece of fabric in the color of your choice
- A needle and thread
- Stuffing material (cotton, wool, or similar)
- Herbs, stones, oils, or other items to use as embellishments or to match your intentions
- Scissors
- Cleansing and blessing tools (such as sage or palo santo)

Steps:

1. Begin by cleansing your workspace and tools with sage or palo santo. This will help to clear any negative energy and prepare the space for your intention.

2. Choose the fabric you want to use for your doll. The color and type of fabric can vary depending on your intentions. Red is often used for love and passion, green for money and abundance, and white for purification and healing. Cut out two identical pieces of fabric into the shape of your doll.

3. Place the two pieces of fabric on top of each other with the wrong sides facing outward. Sew them together around the edges, leaving a small opening for stuffing.

4. Turn the fabric right-side-out. This will hide the stitching and give you a clean surface to work with.

5. Stuff the doll with the stuffing material. Be sure to pack it tightly, but not so tightly that the doll loses shape.

6. Stitch up the opening you left for stuffing.

7. Now, it's time to add the embellishments. This can be anything from herbs, stones, or oils to match your intention. Use a needle and thread to attach these items to the doll, being mindful of the placement and symbolism of each item.

8. Once you have finished adding the embellishments, hold the doll in your hands and say a prayer or blessing over it. Ask your ancestors or deities to imbue the doll with the energy of your intention.

9. Breathe over your doll thrice. This is meant to activate the doll's energy and set it to work on your intentions and prayers.

10. Your Voodoo doll is now complete and can be used in your spiritual practice.

Remember to keep your intention clear and focused while creating the doll, and use materials that match that intention. This will help to ensure that a doll is a powerful tool in your spiritual practice. You can refer to the chapter on the various oils, herbs, and roots you can use for your doll.

Making a Gris-Gris

Materials:

- Small cloth or leather pouch
- Herbs, roots, and/or stones appropriate for your intentions
- Personal items, such as hair or fingernail clippings
- Ribbon or string for tying the pouch closed
- Needle and thread
- Scissors

Steps:

1. Choose a small cloth or leather pouch for your gris-gris. It should be large enough to hold your chosen ingredients but small enough to be easily carried with you.

2. Based on your intentions, decide on the specific herbs, roots, and/or stones you want to use for your gris-gris. You may want to research the correspondences of different herbs and stones to make the most appropriate choice.

3. Cleanse and bless your materials before beginning. You may want to say a prayer or recite a chant for this purpose.

4. Lay out all your materials in front of you, so they are easily accessible.

5. Take the pouch and begin to fill it with your chosen ingredients. Add the herbs, roots, and/or stones and any personal items you want to include. As you add each item, focus on your intentions and visualize them coming to fruition.

6. Once you have added all of your materials, tie the pouch closed with ribbon or string. You may want to knot it several times to ensure that it stays closed.

7. Use a needle and thread to sew the pouch closed, sealing your intentions inside. As you do this, focus your energy on your desires and visualize them coming to fruition.

8. When you have finished sewing the pouch closed, cleanse and bless the gris-gris once again. You may want to recite a prayer or chant for this purpose.

9. Breathe thrice on the gris-gris satchel to activate its power.

10. Keep the gris-gris with you at all times, or place it in a location where you will see it regularly. You may want to recharge it periodically by holding it and focusing your energy on your intentions.

Please remember that these are just basic instructions. You may want to modify them based on your preferences and practices. It's also important to remember that gris-gris and other charms should be used ethically and responsibly with the intention of benefiting yourself and others.

Making a Mojo Bag

Materials:

- Cloth
- Needle and thread
- Your preferred herbs
- Your preferred oils
- Talismans (may include gris-gris)
- Personal effects
- A drawstring or regular string
- Petition paper (paper with your intention written on it)

Steps:

1. First, take the cloth and cut out a rectangular piece. Fold that cut-out cloth in half.

2. Next, stitch the folded cloth on only three sides so that you have one side open. That open side is where your drawstring will go.

3. Turn the sewn bag inside out. Around the open side of the bag, create a seam.

4. Stitch the open seam, remembering to cut out two little holes to allow the drawstring to pass through it. Slide the drawstring in, holding on to it through the bag as you push it till it comes out the other hole.

5. Pick the oils, talismans, herbs, and other things you want to put into the bag. Make sure you're choosing items that match the intention you have.

6. Place your petition paper with your intention into the bag.

7. Breathe thrice over everything in the bag. This is meant to activate the bag's power and set it to work on your intention right away.

8. Pull on the drawstring till the bag is secured shut. Then knot the drawstring thrice.

9. Take the bag to your altar and pray to the Loa and your ancestors that they make your desire come to pass. You may anoint it with oil if you wish.

10. When you're done, place it somewhere out of sight of other people. You may sleep with it under your pillow each night if you wish.

Note that you can use these charms for anything you desire, whether it's finances, health, emotional well-being, protection, provision, increase in spiritual power, getting rid of bad luck, increasing good luck, and so on.

Disposing of Your Charm

When your charm has achieved the intention you set for it, you may want to dispose of it. Here's how:

- First, offer thanks to the charm for all it's done for you. Also, thank your ancestors and the Loa.

- Tell the charm that it's time for it to release the power that it has and stop working. Then light a candle or some incense and burn it by the charm to express your gratitude and release its power.

- When you've finished, remove all the personal effects you've got in the charm, whether it's fingernails, hair, pictures, and so on. You may keep them if you wish or dispose of them somewhere away from the charm.

- Finally, it's time to dispose of the charm. For negative charms or charms meant to get rid of bad situations, you should either burn them or throw them into a running stream or river. If it was a charm meant to bring good things or for good intentions, you can bury it somewhere near a tree to give off its good energy there, or you may burn it if you wish.

Let's Talk Ethics

Ethics are basically the morals that everyone lives by. They're what people use to determine the right choices to make. The codes of ethics differ from one religious practice to another. Still, generally, the common themes include responsibility, respect, justice, honesty, compassion, and fairness. Here are some general guidelines when it comes to the ethics of working with charms.

1. **Please use these charms only for good intentions.** You have to pause and ask yourself if your reasons are justified before you make and use the charms. It's okay to use them for success, peace, protection, love, and things of that nature, but it's not okay to use them to curse or hurt someone, especially if you have no valid reason to do so.

2. **Please do your best to honor the deep meaning of every ingredient you choose to put into the charm.** Once more, revisit the chapter that lets you know the significance of herbs, roots, and colors. You can also do some further research so you can learn more about what's okay to use and how to ethically acquire the materials.

3. **You should always breathe onto your charm.** This will give it life and have it begin working for you. This activation is absolutely vital.

4. **If you come across someone else's charm somehow, please don't touch it or attempt to use it.** If you're curious, seek permission first before asking questions or touching the items.

5. **You should always pray to your Loa and ancestors to let them know what your intentions are for the charms.** Tell them what results you want to get. Trust that they will help you. Keep in mind that you're to interact with them respectfully, so don't try to command them to do things for you. Stay humble, and keep an appreciative vibe about yourself.

6. **You can and should consider recharging your charms.** You can do this by saying prayers over them or by anointing them with oil. You can do this regularly. It's also a good idea to speak to your charm as if it were an actual person because it does have its own consciousness. If the thought of speaking to your charm feels odd to you, you should pause and remind yourself of the fact that all things are created by Bondye, and all things are filled with his light and life. There's nothing weird about talking to your charm. After all, Bondye created you and spoke to you through his Loa — and he doesn't think it's weird.

Working with charms is a powerful way to practice Voodoo and make it a very real thing in your daily life.

So, take a moment to think about your greatest desires. What might you be able to make a charm for? Go for it!

Chapter Ten: Voodoo Spells and Rituals to Try

In the rhythms of Voodoo, there is a sacred structure to the rituals that have been passed down from generations before. As in a dance, the steps are not only felt but known in the heart, and it is with reverence that each movement is made. The four distinct phases of a ritual are:

- Preparation
- Invocation
- Possession
- Farewell

First, the preparation begins. It is a time of cleansing, both of the body and of the spirit. Bathing with herbs and oils to purify the self, sweeping the space to rid it of negative energy, and lighting candles and incense to call in the spirits. This is the time to set intentions and connect with the divine.

Next, the invocation begins. Here is where the spirits are called forth. Each Loa, or spirit, has its own veve, a symbol that is drawn on the ground with cornmeal or flour, and offerings are made to honor them. The veve acts as a gateway for the Loa to enter the physical realm, and through this gateway, they may communicate with the Voodooist. The Loa are not the only ones summoned from the spirit realm. Voodooists also call out to their ancestors to participate in the events unfolding.

Then comes the time of possession. The Loa enters the body of the chosen person, often called the "horse," and through this vessel, they can communicate with the human realm. The horse may dance or speak in tongues, and through this ecstatic experience, the connection with the divine is strengthened.

Finally, comes the farewell. This is the time to release the spirits back to their realm to give thanks for their presence and guidance. The offerings made during the invocation are given to the spirits, and the veve is erased, closing the gateway between the two worlds. In this way, the Voodoo ritual is like a prayer, a song that is sung to connect with the divine. It is a sacred dance, a communication with the spirits that have been present since the beginning of time.

Now you understand the basic structure of spells and rituals in Voodoo, it's time for you to practice some spells and get the hang of things. Let's start with some powerful protection spells. Please don't freak out at the "possession" steps because it's just about letting the energy of your intention, the Loa, ancestors, and all the materials you're working with to flow through you. If you can't feel it, just imagine you can, and visualize it as a beautiful light coursing through your body.

Protection Spells

Shield Protection Spell

Materials:

- 1 white candle
- 1 black candle
- 1 small bag of sea salt
- 1 amulet of St. Michael
- 1 piece of cypress wood
- 1 piece of black cloth
- 1 piece of white cloth

Preparation:

1. Find a quiet and safe space to perform the ritual.
2. Cleanse the space with burning sage or palo santo.

Invocation:

1. Light the white candle to represent the purity and protection of your ancestors and loved ones.

2. Light the black candle to represent the negative energies you wish to banish and protect yourself from.

3. Sprinkle sea salt around the space to purify and protect it.

4. Call upon the powerful and protective spirit of St. Michael to assist you in this ritual. You can say, *"St. Michael, I call upon you to protect and shield me from all harm. Please lend me your strength and courage to face any obstacles that come my way."*

5. Invoke the spirit of Baron Samedi, the Loa of death and protector of the cemetery, by placing the piece of cypress wood on the altar. You can say, *"Baron Samedi, I call upon your power to protect me from any spiritual harm that may come my way. I ask that you bless this piece of cypress wood and imbue it with your protective energies."*

Possession:

1. Take the piece of cypress wood and wrap it in the white cloth.

2. Place the amulet of St. Michael on top of the cypress wood.

3. Wrap the cypress wood and amulet in the black cloth.

4. Hold the bundle in your hands and envision a white light surrounding you, protecting you from all negative energies. Feel this energy taking over your body and mind, "possessing" you, flooding you with its power.

5. Tie the bundle with a black string or thread and place it in a safe and sacred place.

Farewell:

1. Thank Baron Samedi and St. Michael for their assistance and protection.

2. Extinguish the candles and dispose of them safely.

3. Thank your ancestors for their protection and guidance.

4. Sprinkle sea salt around the perimeter of the space to close and seal the ritual.

Bayou Protection Bath

Materials:

- Florida water
- Rosemary (or any protective herb)
- Dried rose petals
- 1 tablespoon black salt
- 1 white candle
- Rosemary oil (or any protective oil)

Preparation:

1. Start by cleansing your bathroom with Florida water or any protective herb like sage or rosemary.
2. Draw a hot bath and add a handful of dried rose petals, a tablespoon of black salt, and a pinch of protective herbs like bay leaves, basil, or mint.
3. Light a white candle on the side of the tub and place a small bowl of water on the other side.

Invocation:

1. Call upon Papa Legba, the Loa who acts as the gatekeeper between the worlds, to open the doors and offer his protection. You can recite a chant or prayer such as, "Papa Legba, guardian of the crossroads, I call upon you to open the way and keep me safe from harm. Let your light guide me through the shadows and keep me protected in your hands."
2. Invoke your ancestors by calling out their names and asking them to offer their guidance and protection during this ritual.

Possession:

1. Get into the tub and let the warm water embrace you. Close your eyes and focus on your intention to be protected from harm, negativity, and anything that might threaten your well-being.
2. Pour a few drops of protective oil, such as rosemary, lavender, or frankincense, on your forehead, chest, and feet.
3. Visualize a shield of white light surrounding you, repelling any negativity and creating a barrier of protection.

Farewell:

1. When you feel ready, thank Papa Legba and your ancestors for their protection and guidance.

2. Drain the bathwater, and sprinkle a handful of black salt around the drain to seal the protection.

3. Blow out the candle and discard the leftover herbs outside of your house.

Note: This bath can be done anytime you feel the need for protection, but it is particularly useful during the waning moon or in times of stress, anxiety, or uncertainty. Use a white candle for purity, clarity, and protection. You can also use other colors that correspond to your intention, such as black for banishing negativity, purple for spiritual protection, or green for physical protection. Use oils that have protective properties, such as rosemary for purification, lavender for peace, or frankincense for spiritual strength. Bay leaves are known for their protective powers, and they also add a pleasant scent to the bath.

For Health

Healing Waters of Loco

Materials:

- 1 white candle
- 1 cup of fresh water
- 1 white cloth
- 1 small pouch with tobacco, mint, and comfrey (you may just use one of these herbs)
- Peppermint oil (you may use eucalyptus or lavender instead)

Preparation:

1. Gather the necessary supplies.
2. Cleanse yourself and your space with a smudge of sage or palo santo.
3. Dress the candle with oil.

Invocation:

1. Light the white candle and place it on a white cloth.
2. Call upon Loco, the Loa of healing and transformation, by reciting

his prayer and invoking his veve with white chalk or flour on the ground:

"Great Loco, spirit of the winds and the trees, I humbly ask for your healing touch. May your gentle winds bring me the soothing balm of your grace, and may your mighty strength transform me from illness to wholeness. Loco, I call upon you to join me in this sacred space, to bless and protect me, and to guide me on the path of healing."

3. Sprinkle Loco's herbs and roots around the candle and the white cloth.

Possession:

1. Pour the cup of fresh water into the pouch of herbs and roots and let it steep for a few minutes.

2. Close your eyes and visualize Loco's energy flowing through your body, cleansing and healing you from any physical or emotional ailment.

3. Open the pouch and pour the healing water over your head and body, letting it wash away any negative energy or sickness. You can recite Loco's name or prayer while bathing in the healing water.

4. When you feel fully immersed in the healing energy of Loco, extinguish the candle.

Farewell:

1. Thank Loco for his blessings and healing power, and bid him farewell with gratitude and respect.

2. Dispose of the herbs and roots in a natural setting, such as a garden or a forest.

Keep the white cloth as a reminder of the healing ritual, and carry the pouch of herbs and roots with you for continued protection and healing.

Loco's Healing Candle Spell

Materials:

- 1 white candle
- Pen and paper
- A drop of bayberry oil
- A pinch of ginger root

- A pinch of hyssop
- A pinch of rosemary

Preparation:

1. Begin by preparing your space. Clear the area of any clutter or distractions, and make sure that you have all the materials you need.
2. Light the white candle and take a few deep breaths to center yourself.

Invocation:

1. Next, call upon Loco by reciting the following invocation:
2. *"Great Loco, spirit of healing, hear my call. I ask that you bless me with your healing energy and restore my body, mind, and soul to full health. I call upon you, Loco, to aid me in this time of need."*

Possession:

1. Take the piece of paper and write down any health issues or concerns you are currently facing. Place the paper in front of the candle.
2. Take a drop of bayberry oil and anoint the candle, starting at the top and working your way down to the base. As you anoint the candle, focus on the intention of healing and imagine Loco's healing energy filling the space.
3. Take a pinch of ginger root, hyssop, and rosemary and sprinkle them around the candle.
4. Light the candle and focus your attention on the flame. Visualize the healing energy of Loco coming through the flame and into your body, filling you with vitality and strength.
5. Repeat the following chant three times:

   "Loco, great healer, I call upon your power.

   Bring forth your energy, in this healing hour.

   Restore my health, and make me strong.

   Great Loco, heal me, and right what is wrong."

Farewell:

1. Once the candle has completely burned down, dispose of the remains and thank Loco for his healing energy.

2. Close the ritual with the following statement:

"As I blow out this candle, my ritual is done.

But Loco's healing energy will continue on.

Thank you, Loco, for your presence and aid.

I am now healed, in your power and name."

This ritual utilizes the white candle, which represents purity and clarity, and the herbs of ginger root, hyssop, and rosemary, which are known for their healing properties. Bayberry oil is also used to anoint the candle, which is known for its protective and healing qualities.

For Finances

Abundant Blessings Spell

Materials:

- 1 green candle
- Chamomile and bay leaves
- Ginger root
- Basil oil
- A small green bag or sachet
- A small piece of paper and a pen

Preparation:

1. Cleanse the space where the ritual will take place.
2. Set up an altar with the green candle in the center, and the chamomile and bay leaves, ginger root, basil oil, and a small bag or sachet on the altar.
3. Light the green candle.

Invocation:

1. Call upon Papa Legba, the Loa who opens the doors to opportunity, with the following chant:

"Papa Legba, guardian of the crossroads,

Hear my call and open the way.

Bless me with abundance and prosperity,

And guide me to success each day."

2. Take a few moments to meditate on your intention of calling forth abundance and prosperity and visualizing the flow of wealth and resources in your life.

Possession:

1. On the small piece of paper, write down your intention and desires for prosperity and abundance.

2. Anoint the paper with basil oil, and place it in the small green bag or sachet.

3. Add the chamomile and bay leaves, and ginger root to the bag or sachet.

4. Hold the bag or sachet in your hands, and focus your energy and intention of calling forth abundance and prosperity.

5. Chant the following:

"Abundance and prosperity flow to me,

Wealth and success come easily.

As I will, so it be."

Farewell:

1. Thank Papa Legba for his assistance and guidance.

2. Extinguish the green candle.

Keep the green bag or sachet on your person or in a safe, sacred space to continue manifesting abundance and prosperity in your life.

Ezili's Abundance Bath

Materials:

- 8 green candles
- Patchouli oil
- Cinnamon powder
- Bay leaves
- Money, preferably in the form of coins

Preparation:

1. Cleanse the bathroom area by sweeping the floor and washing the surfaces with mild soap and water.

2. Set up the green candles around the bathtub, placing them in a circle.

3. Light the candles and turn off any artificial lights.

Invocation:

1. Call upon your ancestors for their guidance and protection during the ritual.

2. Call upon the Loa Ezili Freda, known for her ability to bring wealth and prosperity, to join the ritual and offer her blessings.

Possession:

1. Pour warm water into the bathtub and add a few drops of patchouli oil to the water.

2. Sprinkle cinnamon powder and crushed bay leaves into the water to draw in abundance and prosperity.

3. Visualize yourself surrounded by wealth and abundance. See it in your mind's eye as green energy possessing you, filling you up.

4. Get into the bathtub and soak in the water for at least 20 minutes, focusing on your intentions for financial abundance and prosperity.

5. As you soak, take the coins and toss them into the water, visualizing them multiplying and growing in value.

Farewell:

1. When you have finished, stand up and let the water drain from the tub, visualizing any blockages or negative energies being removed with the water.

2. Extinguish the candles and thank Ezili Freda and your ancestors for their guidance and blessings.

Note: The green candles and bay leaves represent wealth and money, while the patchouli oil is believed to draw in abundance. Cinnamon is used for its energy-boosting properties. By invoking Ezili Freda, you seek the Loa's aid in manifesting wealth and prosperity. Finally, the act of tossing coins into the water is a symbolic gesture of attracting money and prosperity.

For Love

Bain d'Amour (Bath of Love)

Materials:

- 2 pink candles
- A handful of rose petals
- 1 cup of honey
- ½ cup of olive oil
- ½ cup of lavender oil
- ½ cup of cinnamon powder
- 1 red apple
- 1 piece of paper and a pen

Preparation:

1. Cleanse yourself and the bathroom before beginning the ritual.
2. Light the pink candles and place them in a safe location in the bathroom.
3. Cut the red apple into small pieces and set it aside.
4. Write your name and the name of your desired partner on the piece of paper.

Invocation:

1. Sit in front of the candles and take three deep breaths to center yourself.
2. Call upon the Loa Ezili Freda to bless your ritual bath for love.
3. Hold the piece of paper with the names in your hand and speak your intentions for the ritual.
4. Sprinkle rose petals around the candles and on the bathroom floor, creating a path to the bath.
5. Add the cinnamon powder to the bathwater.

Possession:

1. Pour the honey, olive oil, and lavender oil into the bathwater while stirring clockwise.
2. Place the apple pieces in the bathwater.

3. Enter the bath and immerse yourself fully in the water.

4. Visualize yourself in a loving and committed relationship with your desired partner. Speak your intentions out loud or in your mind.

5. Stay in the bath for at least 15 minutes, focusing on your intentions and feeling the energy of the ritual.

6. After you have finished, step out of the bath and let the water drain away.

Farewell:

1. Thank Ezili Freda and your ancestors for their presence and assistance.

2. Snuff out the candles and discard any leftover materials from the bath.

3. Carry the piece of paper with the names on it with you until your intentions manifest.

4. Give the remaining apple pieces as an offering to nature or bury them in the ground.

Note: The candle colors that match the intention of the ritual are pink, which represents love and romance. The herbs and oils that match the intention are rose petals, lavender oil, and cinnamon powder, which all have properties associated with love and attraction. Ezili Freda is the Loa associated with love, beauty, prosperity, and femininity, making her an appropriate choice for this ritual. As with all Voodoo rituals, it is important to call upon one's ancestors for guidance and protection.

For Luck

Lucky Hand Spell

Materials:

- Green candle
- Lucky Hand root
- Five Finger Grass
- Cinnamon oil
- Patchouli oil

Preparation:

1. Set up a clean and quiet space for the ritual.

2. Gather all of the materials needed.

3. Dress the green candle with a mixture of cinnamon and patchouli oils.

4. Place the Lucky Hand root and Five Finger Grass in a bowl or dish.

Invocation:

1. Light the green candle and place it in front of you.

2. Hold the Lucky Hand root in your left hand and the Five Finger Grass in your right hand.

3. Close your eyes and take a deep breath, clearing your mind.

4. Call upon the Loa Ezili Danto, who is associated with good luck and prosperity, by saying:

   "Ezili Danto, powerful Loa of good luck, I call upon you to bless me with your divine presence. Hear my prayer, grant me your protection, and bestow upon me the power of good fortune."

5. Hold the Lucky Hand root and Five Finger Grass up to the candle flame, allowing the heat to release their scents and energies.

6. Take the Lucky Hand root and anoint it with the cinnamon oil, saying: *"As I anoint this Lucky Hand root, I invite the spirits of good luck and prosperity to guide me."*

7. Take the Five Finger Grass and anoint it with the patchouli oil, saying: *"As I anoint this Five Finger Grass, I invite the spirits of opportunity and success to guide me."*

Possession:

1. Place the Lucky Hand root and Five Finger Grass in a small pouch or bag, and feel their energy as you hold the bag in your hands. You can carry it with you for good luck.

Farewell:

1. Blow out the candle and thank Ezili Danto for her presence and blessings.

2. Close the ritual by saying: *"Thank you, Ezili Danto, for your divine presence and blessings. I ask for your continued guidance and protection. I honor the spirits of good luck and prosperity and*

give thanks for their assistance. My ritual is now complete."

These are just a handful of spells you can try out right away. Don't have a certain material? You can always replace it with something else that serves the same purpose. With these spells, you should have an idea of how to create your own rituals for any other purposes you might have that aren't mentioned in this book. It's also helpful to research and learn more about spellwork in Louisiana Voodoo, so your confidence can grow as you practice, and you can have phenomenal results. Do your spells with great respect for the spirits, and be sincere about whatever you need them to help you with.

Conclusion

We've finally come to the end of this book. Now, you know everything you need to begin your journey as a Voodooist. As you have come to the end of this journey exploring the world of New Orleans Voodoo in these pages (and the start of a new one exploring it in your life), you might feel a deep sense of awe and reverence for this profound spiritual practice. Through this book, you have delved into the history, rituals, spells, and religious tenets of Louisiana Voodoo and have been left with a profound understanding of the beauty and power of this practice.

One of the most important takeaways from this book is the importance of sincerity in one's spiritual practice. New Orleans Voodoo is not simply a collection of spells and rituals to be performed without intention or understanding. It is a living, breathing spiritual tradition that requires deep reverence and respect for the spirits, ancestors, and deities that are central to its practice.

You have seen how New Orleans Voodoo emerged from the rich cultural tapestry of Louisiana, combining elements of African spirituality, Catholicism, and Native American traditions. New Orleans Voodoo is a practice shaped by the struggles and triumphs of its people and has given rise to a unique and powerful spiritual tradition.

At the heart of New Orleans Voodoo is the belief in the interconnection of all things. The spirits, ancestors, and deities central to its practice are seen as living entities that can communicate with and guide those seeking their aid. Through rituals, spells, and offerings, practitioners seek to forge a deep spiritual connection with these beings and tap into their wisdom, guidance, and power.

This sense of connection and community makes New Orleans Voodoo a profound and transformative practice. Through your exploration of this tradition, you have seen how it has given solace, guidance, and healing to those who seek its aid. It is a practice that honors the rich diversity of our human experience and offers a path to spiritual growth and transformation.

Approach the practice of New Orleans Voodoo with sincerity, reverence, and respect. Trust in the power of the spirits, and allow yourself to be guided by their wisdom and guidance. Remember that this spiritual tradition requires dedication and commitment, but the rewards are immeasurable.

May the spirits guide and protect you on your journey, and may the practice of New Orleans Voodoo bring you the healing, prosperity, love, and good luck you seek. Walk with grace, power, and love, knowing that all are connected, and the spirits are always with you.

Here's another book by Mari Silva that you might like

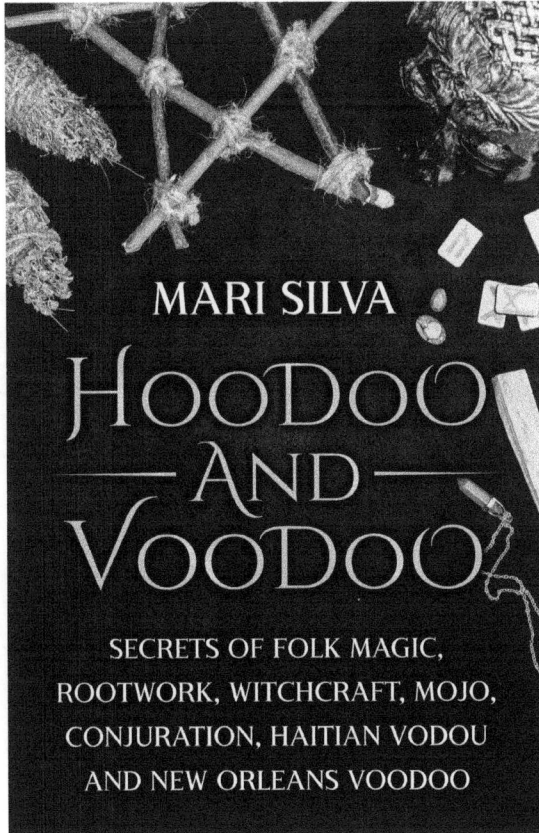

MARI SILVA

HOODOO —AND— VOODOO

SECRETS OF FOLK MAGIC,
ROOTWORK, WITCHCRAFT, MOJO,
CONJURATION, HAITIAN VODOU
AND NEW ORLEANS VOODOO

Your Free Gift
(only available for a limited time)

Thanks for getting this book! If you want to learn more about various spirituality topics, then join Mari Silva's community and get a free guided meditation MP3 for awakening your third eye. This guided meditation mp3 is designed to open and strengthen ones third eye so you can experience a higher state of consciousness. Simply visit the link below the image to get started.

https://spiritualityspot.com/meditation

References

Brown, K. (2001). Mama Lola: A Vodou Priestess in Brooklyn. University of California Press.

Desmangles, L. (1992). The Faces of the Gods: Vodou and Roman Catholicism in Haiti. University of North Carolina Press.

Fandrich, I. J. (2005). The Birth of New Orleans' Voodoo Queen: A Long-Held Mystery Resolved. Louisiana History

Fandrich, I. J. (2007). Yorùbá influences on Haitian vodou and New Orleans voodoo. Journal of Black Studies.

Filan, K. (2010). The Haitian Vodou Handbook: Protocols for Riding with the Lwa. Destiny Books.

Guenin-Lelle, D. (2016). The Story of French New Orleans: History of a Creole City. Univ. Press of Mississippi.

Hebblethwaite, B. (2012). Vodou Songs in Haitian Creole and English. Temple University Press.

McAlister, E. (2002). Rara! Vodou, Power, and Performance in Haiti and its Diaspora. University of California Press.

Murphy, J. (2011). Working the Spirit: Ceremonies of the African Diaspora. Beacon Press.

Packham, J. (2012). Voodoo. The Encyclopedia of the Gothic.

Touchstone, B. (1972). Voodoo in new Orleans. Louisiana History: The Journal of the Louisiana Historical Association

www.ingramcontent.com/pod-product-compliance
Ingram Content Group UK Ltd.
Pitfield, Milton Keynes, MK11 3LW, UK
UKHW021336030225

4420UKWH00005B/281

9 781638 182610